ISBN: 978129035189

Published by:
HardPress Publishing
8345 NW 66TH ST #2561
MIAMI FL 33166-2626

Email: info@hardpress.net
Web: http://www.hardpress.net

"RACUNDRA'S" FIRST CRUISE

BY

ARTHUR RANSOME

First published in 1923

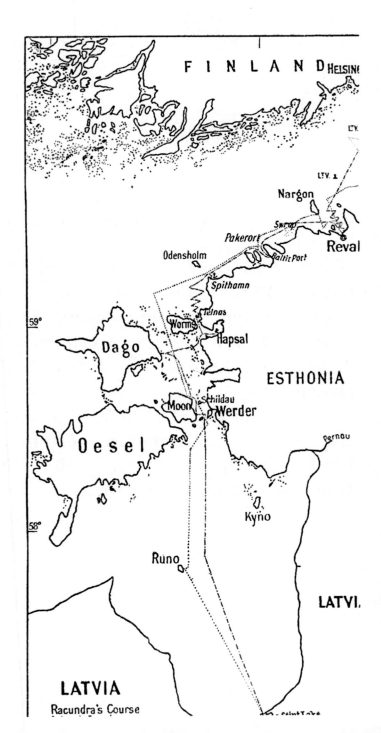

F I N L A N D   HELSING

LTV.

LTV. 1

Nargon

Swrap

Pakerort

Odensholm

Baltit Port

Reval

Spithamn

Telnas

Worms

Hapsal

Dago

ESTHONIA

Schildau

Moon   Werder

Pernau

Oesel

Kyno

Runo

LATVI.

LATVIA

Racundra's Course

AUTHOR'S NOTE

MORE than once in the log of *Racundra's* 1
voyage I have mentioned that I found cha
made by the war unrecorded in the obtain
charts. I have just received from the Estho
Admiralty, through Mr. Edward Wirgo, a se
charts they have recently issued which c
the whole of the delightful cruising ground an
the islands, and should certainly be obta
by the skippers of any other little ships
think of visiting these waters.

CONTENTS

THE BUILDING OF " RACUNDRA " . . . . .

THE CREW . . . .

THE START . . . .

RIGA TO RUNÖ . . . .

RUNÖ TO PATERNOSTER . . . .

THROUGH THE MOON SOUND . . . . . .

WORMS TO PAKERORT . . . .

PAKERORT TO REVAL . . . .

PORT OF REVAL . . . .

REVAL TO HELSINGFORS . . . . . .

HELSINGFORS : SWINGING THE SHIP . . . . .

HELSINGFORS TO REVAL . . . . . .

REVAL TO BALTIC PORT . . . . . .

OLD BALTIC PORT AND NEW . . . . .

THE ROOGÖ ISLANDS . . . .

THE SHIP AND THE MAN . . . . . .

BALTIC PORT TO SPITHAMN . . . . . .

SPITHAMN TO RAMSHOLM

" TOLEDO" OF LEITH . . . .

FROM THE ISLAND OF DAGÖ TO THE ISLAND OF MOON

KUIVAST TO WERDER . . . .

SEAL-HUNTERS FROM RUNÖ . . . . . .

WERDER TO RIGA . . . .

APPENDIX : A DESCRIPTION OF " RACUNDRA " . .

ILLUSTRATIONS

CHARTS

FACING

TRACK CHART OF THE CRUISE . . . . . .

MOON SOUND AND THE ISLANDS . . . . . .

HELSINGFORS, SHOWING NYLANDS Y.C. ANCHORAGE . *Pa*

THE NEW HARBOUR AT WERDER . . . . .

PHOTOGRAPHS

" RACUNDRA " AT REVAL, ESTHONIA . . . *Frontis*

FACING

" RACUNDRA " ON THE STOCKS . . . . . .

" RACUNDRA " LAUNCHED . . . .

THE ANCIENT MARINER AT THE TILLER . . . .

FIRST SIGHT OF LAND (RUNÖ ISLAND) . . . .

WOMEN OF RUNÖ COMING OUT OF CHURCH . . .

INHABITANTS OF RUNÖ . . . .

NYLANDS YACHT CLUB, HELSINGFORS . . . .

GROHARA ISLAND AND LIGHTHOUSE . . . . .

" RACUNDRA " AT HELSINGFORS (AFTER SWINGING THE
      SHIP) . . . .

F

A ROOGÖ WINDMILL   .   .   .   .

ONE OF THE ROOGÖ BOAT-HOUSES   .   .   .   .

SHIPS THAT PASS . . . .

OUR NEIGHBOUR AT SPITHAMN   .   .   .   .   .

TWO SMALL SAILORS WITH A MODEL OF HER   .   .

HAPSAL JETTY (SHOWING LEADING BEACONS)   .   .

DRYING OUT   .   .   .   .

" RACUNDRA " AT HELTERMAA (DAGÖ ISLAND)   .

A HOUSE ON MOON   .   .   .   .

INHABITANTS OF MOON .   .   .   .

THE GATES OF MOON   .   .   .   .

THE OLD RUSSIAN INN AT KUIVAST   .   .   .   .

THE NEW HARBOUR AT WERDER   .   .   .   .

THE NEW LIGHTHOUSE AT WERDER .   .   .   .

SEAL-HUNTERS, THEIR BOAT AND SHIP   .   .   .

THE SEAL-HUNTERS ON BOARD THEIR SHIP   .   .

" RACUNDRA " HAULED OUT   .   .   .   .   .

"RACUNDRA'S" FIRST CRUISE

THE BUILDING OF "RACUNDRA"

HOUSES are but badly built boats so fir
aground that you cannot think of moving th
They are definitely inferior things, belonging
the vegetable not the animal world, rooted
stationary, incapable of gay transition. I adr
doubtfully, as exceptions, snailshells and carav
The desire to build a house is the tired wish c
man content thenceforward with a single anchor
The desire to build a boat is the desire of yo
unwilling yet to accept the idea of a final resti
place.

It is for that reason, perhaps, that, when it con
the desire to build a boat is one of those that can
be resisted. It begins as a little cloud on a ser
horizon. It ends by covering the whole s
so that you can think of nothing else. You m
build to regain your freedom. And always ;
comfort yourself with the thought that yours
be the perfect boat, the boat that you may sea
the harbours of the world for and not find

She was to be a cruising boat that one man
manage if need be, but on which three cou
comfortably. She was to have writing-tab
bookcase, a place for a typewriter, broad
where a man might lay him down and rest w
bruising knee and elbow with each uncon
movement. She was to carry her dinghy o
to avoid that troublesome business of towing
has brought so many good dinghies to thei
end. She should not be fast, but she should b
keep the sea when other little boats were so
for shelter. In fact, she was to be the bo
every man would wish who likes to mov
port to port—a little ship in which, in ter
climates, a man might live from year's
year's end.

Then came friendship with a designer, t
designer in the Baltic, whose racing boats
away prize after prize in the old days bef
war, whose little cruisers put to sea when st
stayed in port. And after that *Racundra*
to exist on paper. There were the lines
stout nose of hers, of that stern, like the
of the Norwegian pilot cutters. On pa
could sit at the writing-table a full yard
in the cabin where (the measurements pro
I could stand up and walk about with un
head. On paper was that little cockpit wh
man, sitting alone, could control the litt
as she made her steady way over the
Then came the sail-plan after how

" RACUNDRA " ON THE STOCKS.

you could keep the sea and keep up to the wi
with mizen and foresail alone. The balance
the sails was such (again on paper) that if you wisl
you could sail under mainsail only, or under m
and mizen, so that you could take down y(
staysail before coming into port and so have
clear deck for playing with warps and ancl
chain. *Racundra*, on paper, grew in virtue dai

It had come to such a pass that I woke fr(
dreams at night sitting in that paper cockpit, w
a paper tiller under my arm, steering a paper sl
across uncharted seas. *Racundra* had to be bu:
There was no escape. But my friend the design
Otto Eggers, lived in Reval, and since the v
has had no yard, or he would have built her hims(
since the two years of paper boat-building had ma
him share my madness. But there was no h(
for it. He could not build. I had to build son
where else, and, since I was to be in Riga, ca:
to terms with a Riga builder.

I pass over as briefly as I may the wretched stc
of the building and the hundred journeys over t
ice to the little shed in which *Racundra* slov
turned from dream into reality. She was to ha
been finished in April. She was promised to 1
on May 1st, May 15th, May 20th and at shc
intervals thenceforward. She was launched, a me
hull, on July 28th. I went for the hundred a:
first time to the yard and found *Racundra* in t
water. The Lettish workmen by trickery got t
builder and me close together, planted us sudder

The ship was launched. Yes, but the sum
over, and there had been whole week
Racundra had not progressed at all while th
and his men did other work. He promi:
that she should be ready to put to sea on Au
She was not. On August 5th I went to
and took away the boat unfinished. N
was setting properly. There were no clea
The centreboard was half up, half down an
stuck. But, under power and sails, som
other, I got the ship away and took her
the lake, had her out on the Yacht C.
removed the centreboard, had a new o:
relaunched her, and just over a fortnig
turned the carpenters out of her and put
But there is no use in reminding myseli
those miserable angry months of wai
remembering the lacquer that was not put
ungalvanised nails that I had laboriously t
from the cabin work and replace with bras:
The hull of *Racundra* was right enough, and
time we had finished with her, we had
the lesser matters that were wrong. Fo
and wise men buy. Well, I shall never bui
and in all probability shall never have
enough to buy. Nor shall I have ne
Racundra turned out to be all that I hac
We took her to sea in the Baltic autumn ;
her at sea when big steamers reported
from the heavy weather, and never for a
did she show the smallest sign of disquiet.

THE BUILDING OF " RACUNDRA "

the rollers on the bar and up the troubled Dv
demure, serene, neat, as if she were returning fi
a day's trip in June.

For those who are interested in such thi
there is a detailed description of *Racundra* at
end of this book. Here it is enough to say t
she is a centreboard ketch just under thirty :
long with a small auxiliary motor. It is a f
horsepower motor, but, possibly on account
my inexperience, it seemed to need forty ho
power to start it, for which reason I did not us
at all during the voyage.

AND now for the crew. There were thre
There was the Cook, to whom, I think, is d
of the credit for the ease and pleasantnes
voyage. She can take her trick at the
need be, but that, for her, is holiday. All t
work was hers. She cooked a meal. It wa
She washed up and, just as the dry dishes
the rack, one or other of that hungry c
would inquire whether or no the time for t
meal was drawing near. She cooked anoth
As its last remains were cleared away, as
fate she would catch the eye of one or oth
looking hungrily at the clock. We, of
navigating, sailing, had our strenuous m
after which would follow long hours of pl
easy steering. She, on the other hand, th
our appetites, became a sort of juggler,
plates, cups, saucepans, kettles, teapot, co
thermos flasks and Primuses in a whirl of p
motion. We, in harbour, idled, fished, and
the barometer and the weather, sustaining
respect by oracular utterance. She, in
as at sea, never for a moment was able to gi

at night, looking down the companion, saw alw
busy hands cleaning obstinate aluminium, and
who rested on his bunk heard, as he turned
comfortable sleep, the chink of crockery and
splash of washing up. The Primuses roa
continually, like the blast furnaces in North
England. And we, relentless and without shai
called continually for food. Of the three of
the Cook, without a doubt, was the one who worl
her passage.

The second of us was the Ancient Marin
On the Stint See at Riga was a tiny harbour
small boats, where during the long months
waiting for *Racundra* I had kept my ding
There, in a little wooden hut on a raft, lived
old seaman, the harbourmaster of this Lilli
port. On my first coming he had spoken a 1
words of English. Gradually, day by day,
language came back to him, and with the langu:
memories of a life he had almost forgotten. Ma
many years ago he had sailed from Southamp
on the famous *Sunbeam* of Lord Brassey.
had spent fifteen years of his youth in Austra
He had shared in the glorious runs of the old
clippers. He had been a seaman in the *Thermopy*
which he called the *Demooply*, and had raced
her against the *Kutuzak*, in which odd Russian:
name I recognised the *Cutty Sark*. And now
was taking care of ten-foot dinghies, and ev
morning made a voyage across the lake in a row
boat with a leg-of-mutton sail to bring the n

varnish, and spoke of her quick passages a
little lake as if she were a clipper returnii
the Horn. He and I became friends, a
before *Racundra* was finished, knowing
had planned a voyage to England, he wei
her in her shed and, returning, begged me
him with me. " I am an old man,"
" and I should like once more to go to so
it is too late." And I, of course, agreed v
for there is no such rigger in the Baltic
Ancient Mariner who has known what it
sail on the *Thermopylæ* in the days of h

Then, as the months passed, and we ki
the builder had made the English voyage in
this year, it was decided that he should cc
Racundra on her first cruise. He spoke of *l*
always as " our ship," and, as we sa:
ambitions for her grew with every day.
we are in the Mediterranean," he wo'
" we must make a canvas double roof for t
or it will be too hot in there." And then,
find the long waves of the Atlantic chil
after this. It won't be till she is near the *l*
coast that she'll have anything as bad
that Ancient Mariner, was on this miniatu
as happy as a boy. Nothing would make h
the ship. He never went ashore, ex
Helsingfors to look for a particular size
maker's needles, unobtainable in Riga,
smaller ports to bring water to refill ou
" Sh   " h   ld   " I h

with a tassel, when he looked like a gnome
pixy or a fairy cobbler. If Queen Mab went
sea she could not find a fitter mariner.

The third of us was *Racundra's* " master
owner," who writes these words even now v
the swelling pride that he felt when he first
them on the ship's papers handed to him
departure by the Lettish Customs Office. " Mas
and Owner of the *Racundra*." Does any r
need a prouder title or description? In mome
of humiliation, those are the words that I s
whisper to myself for comfort. I ask no otl
on my grave.

THE START

On August 19th I got rid of the carpent[
ten o'clock in the evening, and spent th[
part of the night in clearing overboard t[
they had left behind them. A good dea[
mess they had, after the manner of ca[
built into the boat, and I shall not be abl[
rid of it until during the winter I undo [
the work they did. Much of the work th[
supposed to do they had not done, bu[
suffered enough from them, and learnt th[
were prepared to work for another two y[
the boat if I should allow them. If only [
her from them I had to put to sea. The i[
the boat was unpainted, except that I had [
a single coat over the cabin walls and cu[
doing one side first and, when that was dry, [
all the litter across the cabin and painting t[
side. An incredible amount remained to l[
But it was already very late for cruising [
parts, and the last of the yachts that had l[
for summer voyages had returned for th[
before ever we left that little harbour in t[
So, though locks did not work, though th[

THE ANCIENT MARINER AT THE TILLER.

THE START

had only half a dozen blocks worthy of the n
the rest being the clumsiest makeshifts, we l
that if we did not start at once we should not
till next year. We three looked her all over
decided to get away anyhow and finish tl
up on the voyage.

I slept on *Racundra* that night, as I had
for the last two weeks, but for the first time
in a cabin not half full of shavings and carpen
tools. At 5.30 in the morning of August
I jumped overboard for the last time in the :
See and swam round *Racundra* as usual
porridge was cooking on the Primus. An hour
the Ancient Mariner came on board, foll
presently by the Cook. The wind was N
and we were able to slip with it out of the
harbour and reach the whole way down the
to the entrance to the Mühlgraben, which con
the lake with the Dvina River. There was
much wind, and we had time to screw in the c
for the staysail sheets before we had any tac
to do. All three sails were setting abomin:
as we had no battens for them, the builder ha
failed us. I had decided to make the trip to F
without them, knowing that I could there get t
properly made.

The entrance to the Mühlgraben is narrow, ar
tacking through it, *Racundra* refused to stay
ran her centreboard into the mud. We got
however, by pulling the board up a few in
after which there were no more shallows an

the *Baltabor*, was loading in the Mühlgrabe
Captain Whalley, who has known *Racundr*
her birth, since he visited her in the builder
was on the bridge as we struggled by.   The *a*
and I had agreed that two leads were unnec
and had therefore each left his own lead at
so I hailed Whalley as we passed and begg
loan of a five-pounder. *Racundra* went c
zagging obstinately through the narrow
while I tumbled into the dinghy and droppe
and hung on to *Baltabor's* ladder while tl
was found and lowered away to me.   We
often have been in a sore pickle without i

I thought we should probably be all day
through the Customs at the far end of Mühl
and therefore asked Captain Whalley to lu
on the *Racundra* ; and he, who accepted
afterwards have had the blackest thoughts
for, as it turned out, we were held up for or
an hour, and decided to work on to the
Harbour at the mouth of the Dvina, hoping t
our peace with Whalley when we should me
in Reval, where the *Baltabor* was to call.

The Customs House at Mühlgraben is *a*
yellow wooden building, with flowers in the *v*
and a wicket-gate in a wooden paling on the
It stands at the corner where the Red Dvin
the Mühlgraben, and we let go anchor off
the windward side of the channel.   I hu
discarded my disreputables and put on *a*

THE START

difficulty of dealing with officials. *Racundra*
there, a regular little ship, " a proper co
bandist," as she has been described, looking,
her ochre topsides and sharp stern, exactly
anyone of a hundred Baltic smugglers,
her " owner and master " paddled himself as
in the very neatest of new varnished ding
looking as idly rich as he was in reality busy
poor. It was ten o'clock precisely, and as I
given this time in arranging yesterday with
Chief Customs Office in Riga, I felt our punctu
as a sort of moral pipe-clay and, papers in h
tapped at the door of the little yellow house
a most satisfactory confidence. I found the
charming young man who talked English and
me a certificate of clearance without any
He rang up the dock police on the telephone.
harbour policeman, together with a Customs of
from the town, had arrived as the clock was stril
and, everybody being delighted by his own
everybody else's punctuality (the rarest of
things in Eastern Europe), and this being the
occasion on which a foreign-going yacht had l
cleared here, passports were stamped in two mini
another certificate added to the first, after w
all three officials left the little wooden house
me, to visit *Racundra* and, by drinking v
on board, to fulfil the last formalities.

When they saw my dinghy swinging like a
shell below the lofty wooden landing-stage,
refused emphatically to travel in her. wro

on the cabin table before they arrived. V
them bread and butter, ham and vodka, a]
gave us good wishes and the completest]
from the red tape in which, had they
they could have tangled us as spiders tang
Twenty minutes after our first arrival, th(
pushing off again and we were free, our
stamped, *Racundra* cleared for foreign pa
already, as it were, abroad.

Elated by this, we gave only half a tho
Whalley. There was still so much to do on
More cleats to be fixed, backstays rigged
bollards substituted for the sharp-edged
with which she had been disfigured, and x
all for pressing on down to the river mouth
Winter Harbour, where we could lie in peac(
our work and be ready to slip out into tl
the moment the wind should favour us.

We beat out into the broad Dvina River.
was very little current to help us, though I re]
early in the spring the current was so stro
sailing upstream in the *Frida*, a little
cutter, against a local smack, the race was
by the fact that the other boat passed u
first, going backwards, while we were ju
to hold our ground, and that in a good wi]
the water foaming under the bows of botl
On this occasion we were not so fo]
and while we were wearily beating down tl
we were passed with the utmost ease by
racing sloop from Riga, sailed by a friend

wearing high boots and spurs when on his b
He went by at what seemed to be a great sp
and turned into the Bolderaa, a tributary of
Dvina, after hailing us and wishing us good l
" He wouldn't pass us like that if we were at
in anything of a wind," said the Ancient, and
were glad to be comforted, for it is not pleas
to be passed even by a racing boat.

There was plenty of shipping in the Dvina
several coasters were lying at anchor near the mo
of the river, evidently thinking that the north
wind was not done with us yet. The sight
them confirmed us in our intention of stopp
in the Winter Harbour for long enough to get thi
shipshape, and at ten minutes to two *Racun*
after raising our spirits by showing what she cc
do with the wind behind her, when we put the h
up to run back into the harbour, was swinging
her anchor in a good berth near the red rail
bridge.

There were clouds in the N.W. after lunche
but we had a few hours of warm sunshine, a
while we worked on the boat, the Cook went ash
She said that after seeing what we could do v
in the way of luncheon she was afraid she had
enough provisions. We told her that there
a time-honoured rule of the sea : " If grub r
out, eat the Cook." She went ashore in the ding
with little hope, as it was Sunday, but came b
with eggs, black currants, radishes, an ex
hunk of cheese and some more potatoes to f

gimbals set for the Primus stove, and tl
lamp re-screwed on the case of the cer
chain (which runs up through the cal
in a position where it could no longer split tl
by excessive fervour.

But while she had been away the wea
grown worse. Dark enamel clouds in lor
were drifting up ; the wind, still against
increasing, and rain was visibly on its way
us.   A Dane and a German had joined the :
coasters, in the river, and we were ready t
their judgment and spend one more nigh
putting to sea. The Cook started the
The Ancient and I went on with our work
but, nervous for my new sails, I broke ol
the covers on the main and mizen, unshac
staysail sheets, and stuffed the rolled up
into a canvas kit-bag.   I had just finishe
first drops fell. The wind suddenly gre
strong. *Racundra* snubbed at her chai
only once, for we were letting out more cha
she could do it again. And then car
rainbows, lightning, thunder and squalls all t
and we were glad to close the companio
behind us and settle down to a meal in th
and then to smoke and look at charts and
we had not started. It grew dark, and
the cabin windows we could see the light
coasters and the foreigners heaving viol
the swell that came in from the river mo

had told me of such lamentable happenings. '
is better here than in the Mühlgraben," said
" Now, if we had stayed there we should 'a had
put a watch on her all night." He went on
tell a story of a German captain who put his he
out of the deck-house in answer to a call out of
dark, and found a man in a boat alongside, hold
up the end of a rope. " ' Good rope, sir,' says
man, ' and going cheap. I don't rightly kn
myself how much there is of it, but for so mu
I'll sell you the coil.' The captain looks at
rope and sees that it was right enough. He ta
that rope on board, the man in the boat pass
it in to him hand-over-hand. There was a
coil, and he paid for it and turned in. In
morning he calls the mate and tells him wl
a bargain he had made in the night. ' As go
rope,' says he, ' as ever I brought with me fr
Hamburg. Why,' says he, with one foot on 1
cabin floor and the sleep dropping from his ey
' it might be the same rope and for a quarter 1
price.' And indeed it was the same rope, for the
thieves in the Mühlgraben, they had just taken 1
end of the rope off the foredeck and brought
along aft outside and sold it in on board aga
and everybody in the Mühlgraben was telling tl
story afterwards, everybody but one man, and tl
was the Dutchy captain who had made such
wonderful bargain."

RIGA TO RUNÖ

By nine in the morning of the 21st, the
shifted to the west. There was sunsh
in the river, the coasting schooners wer
under way. So we hoisted sails, learnt
windlass was useless, got our anchor 1
and made off out of the harbour for the
the river. A heavy swell was coming in;
still plenty of wind, and we were much
to be held up by a hail from a man on the
House Quay at Dünamünde. We had
that yesterday's ceremony at Mühlgraben
us definitely cleared, but it seemed that
to hand over here the certificate I had
the Riga Customs. The swell was so bi
was more than half afraid of smashing .
against the pier. The man explained b
what he wanted, and we sailed as near as 1
we safely could, wrapped the certificate
with a bit of chain as a makeweight, ai
it on the pier as we cavorted past. 1
grabbed it, opened it, and waved his ha
the river. We were free.

Racundra switchbacked over the swell
only a drop or two of water over her no

d
i
g
i
t
i
z
e
d

b
y

t
h
e

I
n
t
e
r

WOMEN OF RUNÖ COMING OUT OF CHURCH.

however, we put right in a minute or two. .
then, just as we cleared the moles, the wind :
denly fell away almost to nothing, while the s
remained and we rolled about so uncomfort:
that only iron-fastened wills prevented the
sickness of the entire ship's company. It was l
past eleven before we passed the first bell-bi
Half an hour later the wind died altogether,
we wallowed in a dead calm, while the bo
banged impatiently from side to side, and
two mechanical logs (a German and an Ameri
both second-hand and quite useless) which we v
testing one against the other, hung perpendicul
like plummets in the sea. We had a ra⁺
hesitating luncheon, and then, at 2 p.m., the w
which had taken no notice of my efforts on
accordion, gave us another little puff, in respo
I believe, to my rendering of " Spanish Ladi
on the whistle. For two hours *Racundra* poir
north, and when we threw matches overboard
left them undeniably astern. At four we v
in another desperate calm. At 5.30 I bat
and swam about the ship, with Riga li₁
house still in sight bearing south, and the sec
buoy, the " howling buoy," ten miles out bea:
a little west of north. We had a few more sli
puffs and then calm, then a few more puffs,
then, as the sun went down, a little land wind c:
out of the S.E. and carried us at 8.40 past the sec
buoy. We were now fairly at sea, and the w
holding, at 9.20 we boomed out a spare stay

little ship alone in my hands in a night c
dark below and stars above, pushing steadi
into unknown waters. I was extremely
At midnight the wind swung round to th
and for a moment I thought of calling up the
to take the tiller while I shifted sails.
thought I might as well have a try by my
call the others only if I could not help it.
the tiller and handed the boomed staysail
with all the sheets in we were back again
course, close-hauled now, and I was at t
listening anxiously to know if the others ha
my hurried running to and fro on deck.
Racundra had been a sentient thing doing
to help me, she could not have done more t
did. The whole operation had gone lik
work, and the others had heard nothing,
not know of the change in the wind or eve
wind's increase, until 4.30 a.m., when the
came on deck and wondered what I had dc
Riga light, which had seemed close aboar
he had gone down to his bunk.

During the night the binnacle light blew o
and again and finally refused to be relit. I
by the North star, which I kept bobbin;
between the main-top and the peak. Our
had not been adjusted, and a number of l
I had taken on our way out had made il
clear that we had a lot of easterly de
Theoretically our course should have ca

prepared to try it out. After the Ancient came
and took the tiller I hung about the deck to see
dawn, which came up with fiery red splashes (
a nickel sea. With the dawn the wind backed
the S.W., when we eased off the sheets, after wl
I went below and was instantly asleep.

At 7.30 I was waked by a feeling of exciten
on board, and was told that Runö island wa
sight. I ran up on deck to see a low line of t
with a pale red lighthouse above them exa
over our bows. The easterliness of our com
was proved beyond a doubt, for even the Anc
could not suggest that we had been making lee
against the wind. But interest in this techr
point was sunk in our delight at seeing this,
most romantic island in Northern Europe, at wl
we had so often looked on the chart that all sum
had hung on the wall of my room. The spot
the chart, which long ago, sailing further n
in *Slug* and in *Kittiwake*, we had so often prom
ourselves to visit as soon as we should have a
worthy ship, was becoming a reality before our e
I suppose most readers of this book have alre
lost the ecstatic joy of sighting land at sea.
no. I do not believe that even for the ol
mariner that joy can ever fade. It is alw
new, always a miracle, never in the common r
of absolutely predicable events. Islands especi
stir the blood, and Runö, that lonely place, (
fifty miles out from Riga and nearly as far f
the Esthonian coast, with its Swedish seal-hun

but once a year, coming up out of the se
me, sought and found (however incorre
my own little ship, gave me moments of u
able delight. The sunlight strengthene
dark line seen through the binoculars
visible forest. The pale red tower began
to resemble the very inaccurate drawin
which, as a guide to mariners, is tucke
into the drab mainland of the English c
the Baltic. Under the forest appeared wh
and splashes which the Ancient said were
but the glass showed to be sand. Then, as
nearer, we could see the deserted beach
broken-down wooden pier not to be visited
steamer until July next year. There is ar
off that pier in westerly winds, but it is
if the wind blows on shore. Just now the ar
was protected by the southern end of the
and we steered directly for the pierhead.
the tiller while the Ancient worked the le
we sent silent thanks to the *Baltabor* for
it. " Three fathom," called the Ancient.
. . . Two and a half. . . . Two. . . . T
Two and a half. . . . One and a half. . . .'
down with the staysail, in with the sheets
into the wind, and, as she began to go
" *Let go.*" The chain rattled slowly c
Racundra, pulling up to it, had found h
anchorage in foreign waters.

The wooden pier, which was in two pie

cable because of some sudden change of wind
had not been able to come back and claim it be
the islanders had fished it from the sea. Bel
the pier lay sand dunes, behind them enorm
pines bigger than any I have seen even in the for
of Russia, and behind the trees the upper work
the lighthouse, an ugly structure of red iron tu
The anchor and the lighthouse and the wrec
pier were the only things that spoke of man.
shore was deserted. There was not a human b
to be seen. We sounded our fog-horn, think
that maybe they would send out a boat. Notl
happened, and, half doubting if after all we
found the proper anchorage, we unlashed the din
turned it over, and with the spare staysail halye
lowered it into the sea. The Cook and I tuml
in and pulled ashore. The wind showed s
of changing, and we knew that if it veered far
to the south we should have to be off again w
out delay.

Our landing on Runö was like a page f
Robinson Crusoe or a child's dream of desert isla
We rowed in past the broken end of pier and
shallow water, tied up to the rotting timbers
the part of it that ran out from the land.
climbed up and, stepping carefully over the cr
planking, came to the sandy shore. Hummc
of sand rose before us, but north and south of
strip of sand we could see rocks out in the wa
And there, almost on the edge of this tideless
were those gigantic pine-trees growing out o

a felled tree roughly trimmed. But as w
in under those tremendous arches of the
there was an uncanny absence of any
sound. The sand dunes hid the pier. The t
trees hid the iron lighthouse. There was :
but the green-carpeted forest, cloisters for
and that great trunk on wheels exactly lik
that must have been made by the first
wright in the history of our race. Man,
he appear, might be of any kind. Alm
looked up in the tree-tops for pigmies wit
poisoned arrows, and watched the trunks
trees for the feathers of one of Fenimore (
Indian braves.

And then, slowly wandering towards us, k
off the heads of the mushrooms with hi
came man indeed, the Governor-General
Island, a short, lame, elderly man in blue
clothes and a seaman's cap, the keeper
lighthouse, to whom the men of Runö co
a casting vote in all debates. He has no
authority ; no laws confer power on him
it ; but . . . he is the Keeper of the Lig
guardian of the one piece of civilisation i
on Runö by the mainland, the represent
those who do not live on islands, and, I s
tradition invests him with a sort of digni
old days he was sent by a Tsar of Russia
the light on this little island in a sea sur
on all sides by Russian territory. The

Esthonian. The Tsar is no more, and the Sw
of Runö can hardly think with any great hum
of the two little nations which argue, fairly bitt
as to which of them should really own the isl
on which, indifferent to such politics, the Sw
live on, preserving their own life and their
customs in an odd kind of private Middle A
centuries removed from the modern competi
struggle of the continent.

The lighthouse-keeper greeted us. He had h
our fog-horn, and since the people were busy
their harvesting on the other side of the isl
had himself come down to meet us, and to war
that the wind was changing and that we n
soon look to our ship. He knew a few word
English, but more willingly spoke Russian, wl
he knew well, besides, of course, Esthonian
Swedish. He was surprised to see us so lat
the year, and, on learning my nationality, as
with the embarrassing curiosity of foreigners
whom this bit of our mingled foreign and dome
affairs is always hard to explain, " Well, Mi:
and how is it with Ireland ? " This was the
of several such disappointments, for I had hc
in voyaging among these remote islands to be
of politics for once. But I hid my feelings and
him that the Irish were settling their affairs in
Irish way, and then got him to talk of his
country.

I knew already that on Runö competitio
almost unknown. Instead there is a sort of anc

belongs not to the lucky hunter but
community as a whole. The land has been
into workable farms, and if a family incı
cannot acquire fresh land. It merely a
necessary room space to the farmhouse, aı
does not even do that. If a son mar
builds himself a bed, which is set up in tl
of his parents, and twenty years later, if
marries and the grandparents are still alive,
bed is built. You can number the famil
Runö house by counting the double beds
main room. There are two hundred and
persons on the island. The women wear on
the national costume of old Sweden. Con
of church on Sundays (they are devout Lu
they are as uniform as procession of nur
men wear homespun clothes and sealskiı
Their morals are said to be strict. I hav
that some years ago a woman offended
their code, whereupon they tried her by
assembly and condemned her to death.
found, however, that not one of them was
to kill her. So they fastened her in the
of a little old boat and set her adrift in ɛ
The boat did not sink, but was thrown uɲ
Courland coast, and the woman, still ali
found by fishermen, recovered, and, one
to suppose, continued her wicked career
mainland, where people are less critical.
   The lighthouse-keeper told us that peoɲ

these events did not much affect the islande
who had never considered themselves Russia
nor indeed anything else than men of Runö, a
were content to remain so, and to be count
Esthonian, seeing that their business, when th
had any, was with Arensburg; that they caug
their seals on the Esthonian rocks, and that, af
all, the lighthouse-keeper had always been se
from Reval. He took us with him to see]
lighthouse, where he posed for his photogra
very nobly with the lighthouse behind him.
had been higher, he said, but the Germans h
blown off the top of it, besides making a horri]
mess of his house. Civilisation had visited Ru
after all. At the lighthouse we had a drink of fre
water, and then, as the wind shifted definite
to the south, had to give up all thoughts of stayi
longer on the island, and hurried away over t
thick moss under the gigantic trees, picki
mushrooms as we went, and so to the broke
down pier.

We were none too soon. *Racundra* was bobbi
up and down in a manner undignified for her, a
the Ancient had lowered the peak. Where the wat
had been smooth it was already broken. We pull
out in the dinghy, getting well splashed on t
way, hauled it on board, got our anchor, hoist
the staysail, filled on the starboard tack, and we
off for Paternoster and the entrance to the Mo
Sound.

RUNÖ TO PATERNOSTER

IT was half-past one when we got away
we were anxious to take no chances with
on Runö's northern corner, we sailed due
a mile before putting *Racundra* on her
I must point out here that until we
Helsingfors, though our courses were dul
compass, there was very considerable dis
between theory and practice. After th
landfall I allowed a full point for easterly
in the neighbourhood of north, and this p
be about right when, in Finland, we had
put in and swung the ship. But on oth
the error wa seven greater. Our logs also
small use for navigation. Of the two, the
log did not work at all, and the America
we used, was a most pessimistic affair. U
were going at our top speed in half a
registered a little less than two-thirds of the
we actually covered, and, if we were no
and sensibly churning along, the log se
lose heart altogether and registered no
all. I think it had begun life on a mc

The wind was now S.S.W. but continued to ba(
to the south, and at 3.40 we brought the booms ove
It was a fine day and pleasant sailing, and, whatev
the log might say, it was clear enough from our ov
wake that we were steadily moving towards tl
Esthonian coast. The only question in our min(
was, where we were going to hit it and whe
We did a lot ot straightening up on boar
drank coffee by the pint and ate huge qua
tities of food. We were all greatly cheered l
our speed after the dismal experience of yeste
day's calms, ana the Ancient began to thir
we should be in Reval to-morrow and to ta
of record passages.

"One time," said he—" one time I crossed tl
North Sea in twenty-four hours under sail."

"Where was that?" I asked. "Harwich
the Hook?"

"No," said he, with a sail-needle between l
teeth, finishing the end of one of the halyarc
"It was from that place up at the North
Scotland . . . like the Moon Sund, where we'
going."

"Pentland Firth?"

"Ay. Pentland. Twenty-four hours from the
to the Norwegian coast."

"Pretty good sailing."

"And I had my captain sick all the way. Yellc
fever. That was how it was. We were in Mexi(
when he began ill, and I wanted him to go ashoı
But he was Norwegian, and he would have it th

Every day he grew worse. I wanted to
into one of the American ports to put hir
but he wouldn't have it, and was all for
on and getting home to Norway. And
carry on, too. I can't tell you how long we
the passage, but we had a west wind wi
the way, till we were near the Irish coast.
then to put through the Channel, and let
a doctor at Southampton or one of ther
But he wouldn't have it, and, sick as he
a course round by the North of Scotlan
the best way for Norway,' he says. And
through the Pentland Firth, and he was
that I was for hauling our wind and co
Aberdeen. But he would have nothin
And the west wind held and plenty of it,
captain in his fever shouting, whenever I
him, not to take a foot of canvas off her.
made the Norwegian coast in twenty-fou
And then we went into Christiansund, v
was from, and as soon as the anchor was
went ashore, and as he went I told him
ashore and see him in the morning. Bu
not like that. I never saw him again
died during the night.''

I had set a course that, if the error of the
was about what it seemed to be, shou
Racundra within sight of the well-lit coas
west of the Paternoster Lighthouse, so
might learn our exact position in plenty

flash every three seconds. I looked at the cha
which I had spread out on the writing-table
the cabin. No such light was to be found up(
it. I looked again all along the coast of Oes(
No. There was a four-flash light on Laidunin
and nothing else between that and Paternoste
I ran my finger across the chart, which I w
lighting with a little electric pocket-lamp. Awा
to west, far out of our supposed course, near t]
approach to Arensburg, a blinking light was marke
but the period of its flashes was not named.
it were that, then how humbled must be the pri(
of the navigator. I could feel the Ancient waitin
in the dark to hear me, having timed the lig]
by a method (the stop-watch) in which he d
not believe, admit that I did not know wh.
light it was or where we might be. It w:
a most unpleasant moment. So I said nothir
at all.

"What course ?" asked the Ancient.

"E.N.E.," said I, to give myself time. I hढ
just remembered that there was yet hope for n
navigation. We were working by the big Germ£
chart of 1915, the only comparatively large-sca
chart I had been able to get. But in the cha
case was an English small-scale chart covering t]
Riga Gulf as well as much else, and this had bee
corrected up to the spring of this year. I pull(
it out and spread it on the folding table under t]
lamp in the cabin. And, as I looked from yello
splash to yellow splash (lights are marked in th

was marked " 1 flash ev. 3 sec.," with
" 1920." My expanding joy almost lift
cabin roof. I went on deck again a diff
from that cringing, worried navigator
glad that the dark hid the doubt in his 1
some few minutes I said nothing. Tl
all the ease I could assume, I said lightl
were nothing : " Keep a look out for :
light on the starboard bow." By cha:
course we had brought my first treasure
port. " And then," I added, " we sh
another light to port, with a white fl:
second ; and when that turns to red, we :
our course clear for the entrance."

The Ancient answered not a word, l
was a new warmth in the night air
solidity in the floor of the steering-'
various other minor indications of rewa:
fidence. I went below and smoked a m
factory pipe.

We were not moving fast, and it was th
later before we had the other two lig
I was secretly glad we were moving slowl）
confidence or no confidence, I did not wa
too much and attempt the Moon Sound in
In spite of the evidence of the English
was glad enough to have our course cont
meeting at 3 a.m. a steamer going S.V
I knew must have come out of the £
took the hint and altered our course

ourselves exactly in the entrance to the Soun
Paternoster Lighthouse on its island on our por
Werder on our starboard bow, islands and rock
coast stretching away behind us to the south an
west, and before us the Sound itself.

THROUGH THE MOON SOU

THE actual entrance to the Sound is a
miles wide, with the little island of Virela
western side and the larger mass of W
the eastern, each with its lighthouse. The
in some parts of it the shores recede and
are over twenty miles apart, the actua
narrows, twists and turns with such sharp
big ships have more than once gone agroun
attempting a corner too fast or at a time
current was too strong against them.
there are few sections of sea chart on
many wrecks are marked. There is, c
no tide, but the water rises and falls
to the prevailing winds, which also
the direction of the strong current in the
The Russian battleship *Slava* is still to
high out of water on the Kumora Sh
British merchantman *Toledo*, after thr
of waiting, was only last autumn haule
shoal by the Erik Stone. Few British
care to attempt the passage by night, ar
the most careful, who did so venture, lo:
plates from his ship's bottom as his rew:

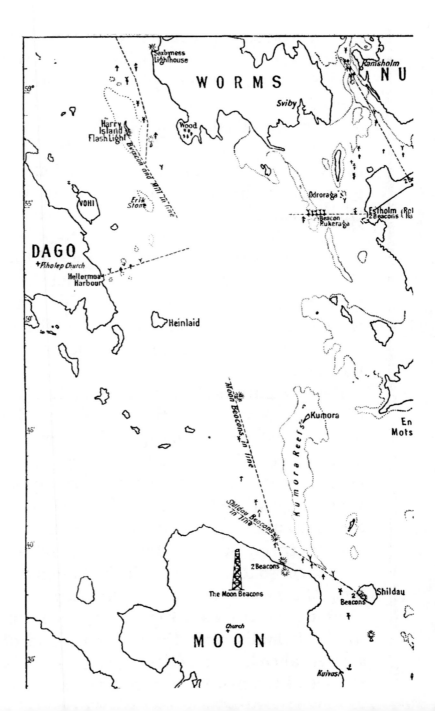

buoys, we could see that we had not only the wi
but also a strong current with us. We had t
most favourable possible conditions. At the sa
time, I was not going to take any risks
Racundra's maiden trip. With our shall
draught we could, no doubt, have cut off ma
corners. We draw, even with the centreboa
down, no more than seven and a half feet. C
good friend *Baltabor*, on her way to Reval fro
Riga, avoids the Sound and goes round outsi
the islands if she draws over fourteen feet.
decided to attribute fourteen feet to the mode
the admirable *Racundra*, and pilot her throu
exactly as if she were a big ship. In this w
we should have ample margin for the correcti
of any errors due to eccentricities of current
the like.

Passing Paternoster, we opened Kuivast on t
island of Moon, a little anchorage where th
is a landing-stage, a coastguard station, an inn a
a telegraph. I had meant to stop there an hc
or two, but the conditions for passing the Sou
were so good that I visited Kuivast only throu
the binoculars. Two or three schooners were
anchor there, waiting for a favourable wind
take them south. The inn looked tempting enou
but, there it was: that glum log of ours w
spinning merrily as a top, the sun was bright, t
wind fair and strong, the wooded island of Shild
showed ahead, through the glasses I could alrea
see one of the pair of beacons that, kept in line ov

bound. So I put the island of Moon re
aside and looked over the bows at Shild.
searched the pale blue windswept water b
for a bell-and-light buoy, which I presentl}
Racundra foamed past it, and I brought it
over her stern with the lighthouse on
Point, the western end of Werder. The sui
the wind blew, and there was the second
on Shildau, at first hard to see, close down
shore under a background of dark-green
And then Shildau was abeam, then on our (
and behold, that dimly discerned second
grew clearer, separated itself from the tree
out, moved slowly nearer and nearer, c]
and at last was in line with the first. Up
board with the helm, over with the booms,
goes *Racundra*, with those two beacons
over her stern, through the narrowest sti
channel, a lane between the shoals close
N.E. corner of the island of Moon. And th
enough on the low green ridge of that islan(
ing at first to be in impossible positio:
straightening themselves out as we sped
were two tall beacons of open ironwork, fa
unmistakable things, each with a dark iro
screw or snake twisting from top to bottc
narrow iron cage. Woods, windmills, green
land, houses, and those beacons, lookii
Mr. Wells's monsters from another planet
over the earth, all changed places in a vast q

were one. The corkscrew of one monster lin
with the corkscrew of the other, the two ca
merged into a single cage, and then, to port v
the helm and sharply, and *Racundra*, shal
the waters from her beloved nose, was off ag
almost at right angles from her former cou
while the Shildau beacons slid rapidly ap
and this new pair remained in magic unity.
took a bearing of the Moon beacons and compa
it with the chart, and got additional confirmal
of the error I had assumed from our Runö landi
That was at ten minutes past eight in the morni
and the log was reading 38.4. Half an hour la
it was reading 41.6, so that even its pessim
was compelled to admit that *Racundra* was do
her six knots.

We were now in apparently open water,
the chart was of a different opinion, and, minc
of our temporary fourteen feet, we kept th
beacons in line for seven miles, when we pas
the light-buoy in the middle of the Sound. Av
to the west was the wide shallow inland sea betw
the islands of Dagö and Oesel. To the east
could see small scraps of islets and knew t
beyond them was the narrow bay of Matsa
from which, more than seven hundred years a
the Esthonians sailed out and away to Swed
and burnt Sigtuna, the Swedish capital, and carr
away its silver gates. After passing the lig
buoy, we held on our course for another sev
miles or so when we sighted the murderous F

red all over by my ingenious friend Captain
with whom, as you shall hear in another
I spent two nights on the wreck of the
aground upon the shoal of which this stone
uppermost point.   Then, the water had been
and there was a little island to be seen, a
birds upon it, but now there was nothing
stone itself.   Far away to the west was th
of Dagö, and, with strong glasses, we could
white house and a red roof by the little l
of Heltermaa.   Far away to the east a fa
iron beacon rose out of the sea, showing wh
the narrow passage to Hapsal between the
of Odroraga and Rukeraga.   We meant to
that way, but we were moving too fast to ha
to spare for dreaming about passages to
There was the Erik Stone; there on the sta
bow the dark woods of the island of l
there, as if floating in the sea, the handful
buildings on the tiny island of Harry; and som
ahead another bell-buoy to be found and
to make the channel along the eastern
Harry and avoid the rocks off Worms.

The sun shone; the wind blew strong
stronger; short, stout little waves raced us,
us, passed foaming and gurgling under ou
and rushed ahead of us to the open Balti
were off Worms almost before we had l
Erik Stone, so it seemed.   And there sho
under the wooded island of Worms we

is one of the Swedish islands belonging to Esthc
In all the harbours along the coasts of this
of the Baltic you meet stout little ships
Swedish names and the words "fran Worm
painted on their broad sterns. You can te
Worms ship at first sight. You have no neec
seek the painted letters. No others have
same combination of beam and lofty freebc
fore and aft. A beautiful sheer these little sl
have, with a high after-deck, the sides of wl
tumble home with an effect no less practical t
lovely—a downward curve to the broad midsl
and then a proud upward sweep to the bows
every line the sense of solidity, breadth, abi
to keep the seas, and an unbroken tradition
simple-minded builders. The ships are mostly ii
fastened nowadays, but the older art is preserv
and I have seen fine schooners, not more t
five years old, in which the fastenings, like timl
and planking, were of wood. For a moment
thought to turn aside, to slip in here under
lee of the island, to make this a stage of our jour
and to talk with some of the little anchored fl
But what would a Worms skipper think of us
we wasted a fair wind? It was not yet noon
the wind showed signs of rising still more. '
barometer had fallen and was still falling. '
wind would hold, and, going at this speed,
should be in Reval before midnight. So Wo
slipped astern and we held on out into the Bal
still among shoals, but with nothing visible

WORMS TO PAKERORT

FOR some time we steered north by west t
a waste of water increasingly disturbed,
south over *Racundra's* stern and keeping
pinewood promontory on the south end of
just open of the slim, gleaming white tc
Saxbiness light on the N.W. corner of the
The wind, now really blowing pretty har(
shifting, and more than once we had to jib
passed one spar-buoy, then another, then
the long-expected light-buoy, and north (
a group of four spar-buoys and a solitar
    Spar-buoys are the loneliest things in t
For those who do not know them I should]
have said before that they are tall posts ar
to the bottom of the sea to mark the sl
On their ends in these parts they carry l
one or two, and according to the number
brooms and to their position, the handles
brooms being up or down, the mariner le;
which side of the buoy is the danger. The
do not long survive the buffeting of wii
water, and these lone sticks with their d
tailed besoms far out at sea have a most mel;

and stood away E.N.E. for the narrow pas:
across the reef that almost joins Odensholm
Spithamn.

The wind strengthened in successive stout brea
and then settled down in the S.E., to blow consi(
ably harder than *Racundra* had yet had opportui
of feeling. We were some eight or ten miles
the land, and the wind, blowing since the aftern
of yesterday, had had plenty of time to get up
waves—nothing, of course, compared to th
there must have been on the other side of the G
but still enough to make a pretty fair test
Racundra's quality. With her broad beam
heavy keel she stood up to the wind magnificen
of course, but, as she dropped between each wa
something fairly thundered within her, shak
the whole ship. It was the centreboard, and
hauled it up, for, with the wind broad on
beam and plenty of it, the difference it made
her sailing (if any, for she is by no means f
bottomed) was fully discounted by the pound
effect on our nerves. Even so we were left w
a noise to which to grow accustomed—
tremendous crashing of the water under her weat
bilge-keel as she sank into the trough. As soor
we knew what it was, we stopped worrying,
before we knew we had crawled all over inside l
feeling her sides, inspecting the boltheads of
three-and-a-half-ton keel, and generally expect
unpleasant surprises. Once we knew what it w
it rapidly became unnoticeable, and we were a

at all.   " She juist joomps out of them
dinghy," said the Ancient, restored to h;
after doubts, during the centreboard's oı
performances, as to whether the keel was
In the general buffeting she got between
the Moon Sound and coming into shelter
land by Spithamn, only one thing gave w
the working drawings for her there had
neat galvanised iron saddle and ring by
gaff jaws, but the builder, saving money, :
bought it, and, at the last minute, hac
wooden jaws, with holes for the lacing bo
too big, thereby weakening a contraptioı
even apart from that was rather ineffectivı
together with screws.   Further, the shrı
the mainmast fell rather far aft, and the ı
being very tall, the gaff tended to swing
and press against the shroud, putting aı
strain on the jaws.   We had heard a lou
aloft, but nothing had come down, and fı
steering-well we could see no damage.
sighting the low island of Odensholm v
lighthouse, and finding the two buoys tha
the passage just north of the promon
Spithamn, where more ships were taking
under the lee of the rising ground with its sı
mills, we heard another crack.   I set a cc
take us north of Sandgrund and the rocks
Spithamn, left the tiller to the Ancient, aı
forward to take a look at things.   I saw

that kept the gaff from breaking loose. This w
pretty unpleasing, but, after watching it for a minu
or two, I became convinced that nothing wou
shift it so long as we held the wind on the sta
board side, which we should do until we came
Reval Bay. In any case we were moving fine
and this place, with Sandgrund, Grasgrund a
the Locust Rock all to be avoided, was not the o
to choose for a stoppage for repairs.

We held on, and *Racundra*, settling down
her work, justified our trust by the speed wi
which she hurried eastwards. At 6.5 we h
Grasgrund abeam and saw the lonely rock, w
out to sea, where in fine weather there is often
broad space of visible ground. On our starboa
bows were the islands of Roogö, off which we h
been becalmed one summer's night in *Kittiwa*
There was Pakerort Lighthouse, tall on its cli
the witness of how many of our struggles in t
recalcitrant but lamented *Slug*. In the bay
the hither side of Pakerort was Baltic Port. I
were already in familiar waters. And, with t
thought of Baltic Port, our pleasant anchorage
last summer, came doubts as to the wisdom
standing on for Reval in the dark through wh
in any other boat we should have called a stor
with so serious a piece of trouble as broken g
jaws awaiting attention aloft. We should ha
to beat into Reval Bay anyhow, when the g
jaws would infallibly come down. It would th
be dark. Better beat into Roogowik to Bal

the helm down for a moment, and sto‹
hauled into Roogowik.   But we were alr
late.   The deep bay running S.E. into
left us again without protection, we were k
into a head sea, *Racundra's* speed fell off,
twilight was upon us.   It became imperativ
a look at those gaff jaws while it was :
enough to see.   The Ancient lowered away i
which stuck, of course, in the makeshif
then loosed the throat halyard, when tl
thing came down in a tumultuous and e
rush.   Within a minute we had learned t
her staysail and mizen setting as badly as t
were, *Racundra* would have a very diffic
beating against a heavy sea under those
alone.   She absolutely refused to stay (
to explain that now, when we have pu
right and given her the tackle she deser\
generally clearing up the abounding erroi
rigging, she stays with the utmost reg
We had to wear her each time we wen
Now, Roogowik is a narrow inlet deep i
shore, but with rocks along both sides
awkward reef running out north of the
which is well into the inlet on the east‹
It grew perfectly dark.   The harbou
appeared, but there were no lights wha:
the Roogö island shore opposite the
We could not tell how near we were to
when on the tack that took us in that c

found ourselves not snugly making repairs
Baltic Port, as we had hoped, but rushing wild
in the dark from one side to the other of the ba
desperately wearing round when we thought ʋ
could afford to go no farther, and gaining absolute
nothing in our struggle towards the green lig
which meant, as I thought then, a well-knov
harbour.

Providence, perhaps, was with us, for, as ʋ
were to learn a fortnight later, if we had gone
there with the wind behind us, as it would ha·
been if only we could have made the entranc
which is from the south, we should almost certain
have been smashed up. The harbour had be
halved in size since last year. The open spa
through which I should have tried to go to my o
anchorage had been blocked by a new pier of bla
tarred, timbers, quite invisible at night, and m
old anchorage, behind it, was high and dry o·
of the water. I do not like to think of what wou
have happened if, with that wind, we had rac
into that blind alley in the dark.

However, we had no chance of doing any su
thing. With the darkness the wind increased ·
a gale and our position became rather serious
uncomfortable, for it became clear that, so f
from gaining, we were actually losing groun
and that with each tack we were coming near
to the reef instead of farther into the bay beyor
it. At this point, the Ancient and I had o

to give us a chance of doing anything b\
anchor, and that if we got anywhere\
shore, unless actually in the harbour n\
should infallibly go on a rock. I was\
for admitting that Baltic Port was a\
for wearing for the last time, getting\
into the middle of the bay and clear of\
and then putting the helm up and runni\
sea until beyond the precipitous point of\
when I should bring her up to the wind a\
so till morning. There was a little\
bitterness on the subject as we shoutec\
other and tried to hear what the other was\
back, and it ended in *Racundra* pretendin\
never wanted to put her nose into Balti\
all. She stopped bucketing into the w\
with sudden restfulness and three times t\
flew out of the bay with the wind at he\
the open sea, where she was more at ho\
Ancient watched Pakerort light till from\
top it looked down over our stern, and t\
below and to sleep. There was, after all\
more to be done.

PAKERORT TO REVAL

THEN began a wild but, in a curious way, rath
enjoyable night. No misfortunes at sea are enjo
able in themselves. He is a liar who says they a
and he is a fool who courts them. But wh
misfortune has come against your will, when it
there, when you have shaken hands with
realised it thoroughly, and done what you thii
is the best possible thing to do, there comes
sort of release from further worry which is qui
sensibly pleasant.

There was *Racundra* with her mainsail gon
proved incapable of beating under staysail ai
mizen, rigged as they then were in a tempora
manner, careering through steep seas in a pitc
dark night with no sidelights and a binnacle lan
that would not burn. On the face of it, miser
Yet there was no misery about it. While in th
narrow bay I had been much afraid, but here,
the open sea, things were much better. Beside
we were doing the thing which I had myself urg
as the right thing to do. It was my own thin
this careering business out here in the dark, ai
I had the joy of possession. I was still afraid.

working sideways to Nargon island, and
headway if possible towards the shallov
this side of Surop, without going on the
the near point of it and without getting
bay until it was light enough to see what
about. Wind and sea had clearly made
minds to knock us and blow us to Fin
if we insisted on working sideways, to
on Nargon like many good ships b(
Racundra and I were of a different deter;
and, as we careered in the dark over wav
always seem bigger at night, I had th(
impression that *Racundra* was enjoying
in her fashion. I found myself, who do
in happier moments, yelling " Spanish
and " Summer is icumen in " and " Jol
at the top of my voice. Then the Cook
up the companion way with a sandwi
asked, with real inquiry, " Are we goir
drowned before morning ? "

I leaned forward from the steering
shouted, " Why ? "

" Because I have two thermos fl;
of hot coffee. If we are, we may
drink them both. If not, I'll keep one
morrow."

We kept one. We drank the hot cof
the other and ate a huge quantity of sar.
The more we ate the better things seem
grew accustomed even to the din. D

as calmly as *Racundra*, and like *Racundra* w
enjoying it, fell asleep in the middle of a laug
She was tired out, and when the next big spla
woke her, I sent her below to lie down, knowi:
that there would be plenty of work for her in t
morning, whereas there was nothing she could w·
do at the moment. I do not believe she h
forgiven me yet.

After that, Pakerort light and Surop light a1
the far-away flash of Nargon were my companior.
The riding light, the only one of our lamps th
would burn except the swinging lamp in the cabi
I had under my knees in the steering-well. Wi1
an electric pocket-lamp I had a look at the binnac
now and again. So we went on, hour after ho1
until I too fell asleep.

I suppose everybody who has spent long hou
at the tiller of a little boat has done the sam
But, I admit, I was startled the first time I wo1
to find myself in the steering-well of *Racundr*
holding a kicking tiller, with the dark in my ey·
and a great wind in my face. The next time
happened I said to myself, " Done it again !
and began pinching myself as hard as I coul·
in muscles, in any places that seemed to hur
in the effort to keep awake. It was no use. T1
lamp was burning all night in the cabin and lig1
came up through the round windows in the cabi
roof. I had shifted the riding light from the floc
of the steering-well to the seat behind me. ·
faint. divided light was thrown on the staysa

wrestling with a large and difficult collar-s
in a stiff shirt, and only slowly came to u
that the collar-stud was the tiller and
shirt spreading somewhere before me
lonely staysail. A minute or two later tl
was the moulded base of a huge table
staysail was a corner of tablecloth most ai
put on crooked. " Do put that cloth
I woke saying, and found myself, as befor
Racundra up into the wind.

I think that is the secret. One coul
to sleep at the tiller with the wind aft, l
close-hauled, steering is done so much
especially in the dark, that the ship tak
the sleeping helmsman. I never once v
sails flapping, and never once to find tl
fallen off the wind. *Racundra* took ca:
skipper, who was far too tired to take
himself. Then, suddenly, the sleeping f
from me and I was extraordinarily awa
unpleasantly aware of what I took to
martial idiot rushing about with a li
of war showing no lights but the c
disconcerting flash of a projector. Th
the lights of a steamer from the west (a:
afterwards, our old friend the *Baltabor* fr
also at that time, when we were bucketi
without sidelights, a thing of infinite ha
then, suddenly, with a relief which let
how great the strain had been, I knew
eastern sky was distinguishable from

PAKERORT TO REVAL

Day came, or the light before the day, and
found exultantly that I was now not sleepy
all. We had done much better than I had expect
in the dark. We were well clear of Nargon ar
about two miles from Surop. I held on joyfull
no longer thinking of calling the Ancient, who
last, when the sun was up, came on deck and, wi
that little faith of his, as once before he had look
for Riga, now looked for Pakerort. Everythi
was hope. We could see what we were doing, ar
the Ancient dug out the trysail from the sol
mass of gear and sails stowed in the forecas
during our hurried departure. We disentangl
a halyard and got the trysail up, wore ship aft
an ineffectual attempt to go about, and stood
on the port tack for Fall and the hollow of t
broad bay west of Surop, to get under the shell
of the land for repairs that would let us hoist t
mainsail again, without which we were so bac
crippled. At last we got into fairly smooth wat
We drank the hot coffee from that other therm
flask. The Cook worked one of her miracles a
produced great bowls of porridge. The Ancie
Mariner made a wonderful job of a manilla ro
substitute for gaff jaws. This done, the Cook to
the tiller while we took off the trysail and hoist
the main. Would it stand or would it not?
stood most beautifully, and with singing hea
we went about and on the starboard tack, clear
the rocks by Surop and then, coming nearer

momentarily backed to the east. We st
Zigelsko Bay.   Reval was in sight for a
then blotted out by big rain squalls.
about thinking to clear Karlo, but the win
too, and had such strength that even wi
mizen it took all the strength I had to kee
the point, which she seemed determined
I ran her off a little whenever I got a cha
there were moments when it was impo
do anything but luff, and Karlo, now a
invisible in the squalls, seemed most unp
close.   These squalls were, I think, the
wind we had throughout the storm, and I
forced over by them, and meeting the sh
waves of the entrance to Reval Bay, ship
water than throughout the whole of the re
passage.   The Ancient had left the forecas
open under the overturned dinghy, and
Cook, guessing what had happened, went
and closed it from underneath, each w
came over sent a deluge below.   Holdir
the cabin in a sort of whirlwind of flyi
pans, apples, pipes and other loose lun
Cook was persuaded we were going to
bodily under water, but *Racundra's* a
nose took care of that.   We had a
exhilarating time clearing Karlo, after w
squalls slackened, and we stood righ
the bay towards the low hill and wind
Miderando, went about there, and tack

shelter and finding things easier, until at last ᴠ
rounded smoothly into the harbour, picked up
buoy, warped into a berth by the Yacht Cl
Mole, made all snug and had a pretty decisi
supper.

PORT OF REVAL

I SUPPOSE it is as true as many things in
that Linda, with whom Esthonian chronicle
was born from a grouse's egg. She refused
and the moon in marriage, giving them the s
categorical reasons for their rejection, and
instead the young giant Kalev, who, after
days' wedding feast, drove off with her in h
and came to this wild country by the s
Their son, the Kalevipoeg after who
Esthonians name their ships, cleared part
country from rocks and made places fit f
growing and pasture, slew all the wild
took part in the struggles of his people
the Christian invaders from Germany, an
in hell with his fist stuck fast in the c
thereof. The old giant Kalev died here a
and Linda heaped stone after stone upon h
and so made that proud hill of Reval by th
Sea, to carry in stone and mortar the r
over seven hundred years of Esthonian
Up there on the skyline are fortifications
the Danes. There are walls and towers 1
the Swedes. The old town hall under the

them with the old portraits of the burghers s
on the walls; up on the hill-top the houses of t
barons, and over all the monstrous gold-don
Russian church, breaking with a touch of Byzanti
the Gothic and Scandinavian outlines of the pla
But for the Russian church, Reval is in colou
little like Shaftesbury; in form its rock is a lit
like the rock of Edinburgh, if only that were
in a plain on the edge of the sea. Most of
it is like those night-cap-country towns that
old German wood-engravers used to put into tl
backgrounds.

But I know Reval too well, and like it too mu
to be able to write of it with the aloof ease tha
only possible in writing of chance acquaintar
ships with towns and people. Sailing in ther
always, for me, like coming home, and I har
know how to give a picture of it, as if I were see
it for the first time.

Coming in as we did on this occasion in a se
of rain squalls, there was little of the town to
seen; but going home to the hills a man does
feel their presence the less if the tops are veilec
clouds. Everything in the harbour was an
friend. There were the little tugs, the *Kalev*
the *Walter*. How often their wash had aln
rolled me off the roof of *Kittiwake's* cabin, on wl
I used to sit here in the evenings watching
ships! There was the old grey elevator that so
how, though modern, carries with it a suggest
of Danzig and the Hansa towns, rising high ab

poeg, busy as usual on their regular trips to
and Stockholm. The same old motor-
the Yacht Club Quay was undergoing t
old repairs, and even the buoy to which
fast was one into which I had often bu
bringing the erratic *Kittiwake* home a
Why, *Kittiwake* herself, unkempt, dila
lovable little thing, was moored just on t
side of the mole.

The stranger going ashore for the fi
at Reval from his little ship need ask
guide than the castle rock. Leaving the
he has but to follow the road that leads
the hill and he will enter the town as it s
entered, through an old stone gateway
by a tower, with stout and lofty stor
stretching to right and left. He will th
on a cobbled street or on a very narrow p
under ancient houses until he comes to the
the rock. He can then walk by a zigz
up the face of the cliff, but if he is wise, ar
not spoil what is before him by preliminar
he will keep on under the walls till, through
street, he comes to another fortified gatew
going through that will climb a long slop
the inner wall until he comes by the
Russian church to the upper town, as it i
built on the summit of the fortress.
the old house of the Russian Governor
the Esthonian Parliament meets. Still

age that they stretch across the road and se
to try to sweep the opposite pavement. Turn
then down a narrow lane, going through an ar
way, crossing a yard and going through yet anotl
arch, he will come out upon the battlements a
have before him the finest view to be obtained
any of the Baltic capitals. He will be look
down sheer precipice on the ancient walls of
lower town, with the round grey towers that 1
above them and the tall dark spire of the chu
of St. Nicolas of the sailors, and far over the ro
of the town he will see the harbour with the sh
coming and going about their business, wl
before him lies the great stretch of the blue b
steamers lying in the roads, white-sailed yacl
sedate schooners slipping away northward
Finland far beyond the little island of Wulf,
moving westward between Nargon and the m:
land, where again is open sea and clear horiz
. . . I cannot believe that any man who
looked out to sea from Reval castle rock can e
be wholly happy unless he has a boat.

My imaginary wandering freemason of the
warmed by the thought that he has a share
all this, that he too can sail past those dist
promontories, since his little ship is awaiting
in harbour, will then go down from the bat
ments by the rock path until the sea is hid
from him, but only for a moment. He will c
the railway lines and come out on the stony f
shore, where he will find a little square harbour

salve their pain by hiring boats from oth
Here, too, he can listen with amusement
buying and selling of every sort of sma
which goes on with all the cheerful mend
a horse-fair. This is the last refuge o
discarded from the Yacht Clubs, and here
of ancient ruins are given a coat of pa
bought by the unwary and sold by the
who know that those who have looked f
battlements above them must have a boa
On the foreshore men are always at work 1
little ships, and you may find there illu:
for a whole history of Baltic boat-building
a year ago I saw here one of the early
boats that were brought from the upper re
the Volga, a flat-bottomed boat with plan
together with strips of leather. In old da
boats used to be brought to Reval by fi
from Ostashkovo, in the interior of Rus
came for the summer fishing season, so
fish and their boats here, and bough
Esthonian horses with which they retu:
sledge overland in the winter, to build ne
and come again next summer.[1]

But if castle rock and stretching bay and
disreputable foreshore are among the glo
delights of Reval, they are not the tow
which, clustered about the foot of the ro
of all the Baltic capitals, least of the vi

[1] Not far from here, in a river farther along th
have seen a quite new dug-out boat, like the boats of

town and most of the virtues of a village. Nobo
in Reval tries to dress well, with the exception
a few young women, and they, by the manner
their failure, do but emphasise this cardinal virt
of their native place. Top-hats were unkno'
there until the British Consul and Vice-Con:
spread awe and astonishment by wearing them
state occasions, thereby startling the Minist
into ordering at least two from England, for t
use of the Cabinet. Not that for a moment
would be thought to laugh at men who had t
courage to carry through a foreign policy agair
the almost open threats of greater Powers, and ha
had the satisfaction of seeing half Europe foll
at their heels. I do but lament the introducti
of those four top-hats and recognise that we, a
not the Esthonians, are to blame for them. Anywe
they are very seldom to be seen, and I think th
after that first moment of horrified exciteme
everybody has come to realise that Reval is n
the place for them. In Reval nothing is done i
show, except, perhaps, an occasional march
troops or fire brigade. And that you must ha
in any capital. There is no single street in Rev
given up to fine shops and the parades of foo
Everything is decent, homely and unflurried.

There are shops, of course, but the buying a:
selling in the town is for the most part done
the older manner. The Reval housewife does n
go shopping for her day's provender. She go
to market with a big string bag in summer ar

market, and beside it little wooden booti
you can buy string bags or even baskets
your food in, doormats to wipe your feet
you get home (I bought one for the
Racundra's visitors), and saucepans in
cook it after you have arrived. The
is made up of rows of tables on trestles, e
a little roof. By old tradition, the sellers
particular kind of goods keep together.
way they can keep a check on each other
and you, interested in quality, can com
cabbage with another or prod the breast
a dozen chickens on different stalls be:
make your choice. In one part of the
you may walk between rows of boxes full
some of them still alive in bath-tubs, t
(two- and three-pounders are not the ra
they are at home) and baskets full of
shining *killos*. In another part of the
you are among green vegetables. In
you buy hunks of meat wrapped in F
newspapers and dripping blood and prin
At one side of the square are the little cai
have brought all this food in from the sur
country. And there is a row of booth
as you pass, you hear the loud cheerful
people drinking tea with great pleasure,
of sugar between their teeth, and there
farmers and their wives, sitting by the
on the trestle tables, eating enormous c
of sausages. Besides this market there is

inhabitants of Reval, and they ought to kno
Both markets are in perfect keeping with t
mediæval character of the town.

*   *   *   *   *

Racundra lay five days in Reval, while l
designer examined her all over inside and out
see what the builder had made of his dream, a
set himself to put right as many as possible of c
makeshifts. He made a new horse for the ma
sheet to work on, gratings for the seats in t
steering-well and battens for the sails, besic
putting on the best of his old workmen to rep.
our damaged gaff. Meanwhile we bought wł
we could of the things we needed, but finding tł
there were no blocks in Reval to fit our ropes,
decided to sail over to Finland and to finish c
fitting out in Helsingfors. We rigged a yard i
our squaresail, but found that the sail was t
small to be of real use. The making and mendi
took time, and meanwhile the S.E. wind th
would have carried us to Finland in a few hoι
was blowing itself out day after day.

We had plenty to do, of course, as one alwa
has in even the smallest of ships. The gangw.
plank that we had rigged up over the stern w
continually trodden by *Racundra's* visitors. Ꮃ
too, had many friends to see in the town, and nc
and again went visiting in the dinghy in the harboι
Baltabor was there, having got in the morning
the day that we arrived and Captain Whall

away with the instrument on board. Th
was another English ship in the port, t
of Erin, a fine Bristol Channel pilot vesse
rigged, which had taken a cargo of]
Petrograd. Her owner was a true n
adventurer, who told us that his real
was the breeding and selling of polo ponies
out wishing to hurt *Racundra's* feelings, w
a little the broad decks and roomy hol
Maid of Erin. She was three times our
of course, black and piratical in appeara
what a ship to make a home of! Her c
the other hand, had plenty of admira
Racundra, so we parted with mutual good
made still warmer on our side by a present
Maid of Erin, whose owner hailed me a
rowing back in the dinghy from getting m
cleared for Finland, and handed down a
plug tobacco, worth to me then many
weight in gold. The Ancient and I s
between us, and often, as we smoked,
" that fine black pirate ketch " and w
if we should meet her again. She was go
we returned from Finland.

REVAL TO HELSINGFORS

On August 30th, when we had our new gaff ja~
and had put the battens into the sails, we we
impatient to be off. The Cook remained in Rev∢
making room for my friend Mr. Wirgo, who at o:
time represented Esthonia in London and h∢
arranged to make the passage with me to Finlan
In early youth he spent some time on a sailiɪ
ship, and now owns the *Condor*, a little Swedi:
yacht, delightful in sheltered waters, but n
fit for the crossing to Helsingfors. We had sail∢
round the harbour in *Condor* the preceding nigɦ
when Wirgo managed to tumble into the wat
while getting into a dinghy. The unfortuna
effect of this was that when we had already start∢
for Finland he complained of feeling ill, and aft
being dosed with aspirin from *Racundra's* medici:
chest, had to spend most of the passage in ɦ
bunk. At the start, however, he was mo
impatient to be off, and was anxious that we shou
use the engine, which, however, was determin∢
not to be used. He explained that, whatev
happened, he must be back the day after to-morrɑ
in order to take his wife to a ball in honour of tɦ

a magnificent piece of work, for *Racundra* is
little ship, the illness began which last
we were already within sight of the Finnis
We started in the evening in the hope o
a land breeze through the night, and this
though the breeze was so slight that when
broke we were still close to the island
which protects the Bay of Reval from th
I steered all night until the dawn, which
clear of the bay. It was pleasant work
admirable leading lights of Reval as a gu
I took a number of bearings which c
the deductions made already about the
character of our compass deviation. By
six we had passed Nargon and Wulf, and
we could see Wrangel island, east by nc
on the horizon the Revalstein three-mast
ship a little north of N.W. The wind dr
nothing. It had only needed the dottir
i and the crossing of a *t* to make it nothin
We were simply drifting.
And then, quite suddenly, came the fog,
it the slightest possible breath from th
veering now and again. We steered, c
pointed, for the ship could hardly be c
as under sail, N.E., E. by N., and E.N
fog was a white, cool fog, and hid everyt
the water within a few yards of the sh
Ancient Mariner brought up the fog-horn
the proper intervals we made the noises p

at the wheel in turns. There was somethi
uncanny in being unable to see in a fog so whi
so luminous in itself. Yet there it was, su
enough fog, as Huckleberry Finn would say, a
we began to be worried by noises. Once or tw:
there were good recognisable noises made by otl
vessels : to these we cheerfully replied, proud
the fact that we could do as much ourselves. T
worrying noises were the regular ones, signa
from lighthouses, lightships and similar thin;
which we ought to have been able to identify ai
could not. The fog lasted until four in the afte
noon. For some time before that the wind had be
easterly, such as it was, and we had been pointii
north. We had heard one particular noise whi:
had disturbed us very much indeed. Hoots ‹
a fog-horn and then the clear ringing of a be
repeated accurately at three-minute intervals. No
when a ship moves at all, the desires of those ‹
board tend to make them believe that she is movii
faster than she is in fact. Although, until we hea
these signals, somewhere to south of us ai
seemingly quite near, we had supposed *Racund;*
was about half-way across the Finnish Gulf, y
when we heard them, it never for a moment occurre
to us that they could be anything but signa
from some lighthouse or lightship standing f:
out from the Finnish coast. We accordingl
searched the *Baltic Pilot,* and examined the Finnis
coast in both English and German charts, tryin

ward as swiftly as it had come, disclosing
absolutely naked to the north and bal
south except for a three-masted ship
sails and with curious swellings about tl
the Revalstein lightship, which we had
to be quite twenty miles astern.   It was
long afterwards that, idly looking over
of the Esthonian coast, I realised that t
minute bell we had heard when wrapp
that blanket was from the Kokskar Ligl
few miles east of Wulf.

With the lifting of the fog came a wind
N.E. which allowed us to sail northwards,
as navigators but renewed in hope a
beings. We knew now where we were,
wind was taking us, not quite in the di
which we wished to go, but pretty nearl
direction. The only thing remaining
was the deviation of our compass, and t
regard to that, we had a good deal c
knowledge in place of the complete ignor
which we had started from Riga. Late
confidence was increased by the sight o:
masted schooner also sailing north. She
sails full and was going at a great pac
overhauling us, but when she passed t
obvious that she was making much mo
than even the generous *Racundra* allowe
We were sure that she too was bound for H
or at any rate for a sight of the Aransgr

NYLANDS YACHT CLUB, HELSINGFORS.

sight of the light-vessel, which we knew must l
somewhere a little east of our course. In th
way, navigating very much from hand to mout
we took the schooner as our guide and stood (
as she had done, until at the same moment tl
Ancient sighted land ahead and I saw the ligh
vessel about five miles distant on our starboa:
bow. We stood on till we thought we could fet(
the vessel on the other tack and then went abou
just as dusk was falling, when we received a
extremely disconcerting shock.

"It's the Aransgrund light-vessel sure enough
I had said, inspiriting myself, and added, by wa
of giving the crew and passenger some confiden
in my knowledge to replace that which they ha
lost owing to the unfortunate reappearance of tl
Revalstein: "She will show two red lights, o1
from each masthead." I had just got this inform
tion from the *Baltic Pilot*.

Dusk fell. We were all on deck, looking f
those red lights. And then the vessel showed 1
red light of any kind, but a white light that vanish(
and reappeared, one of those called " occulting
on the charts and in the light lists.

"It isn't the Aransgrund, after all," said tl
passenger, but the Ancient supported me out
esprit de corps, and I, for our very honour, held
it that it was, in spite of the visible fact that
showed a white light instead of two red ones.
plunged down below and looked it up once mo

at all, I looked at the only other chart I h
was a small sketch of the minefields at
a little book of *Notices to Mariners* giv
by Captain Whalley of the *Baltabor*. 1
sketch chart in general showed no details
detail that it did show fairly glowed before
" Aransgrund Lt.V.   White occ."   The l
been changed.   It was the Aransgrund li;
after all, and I returned on deck with
in my hand, my authority as navigat
reinforced by the printed word of th
Board of Trade.   It was a proud momel
had no time to enjoy it, for with the da
fell suddenly upon us came a great win
the east, and *Racundra*, who had m
day upon an even keel, was suddenly g
much as she wanted.   We could not f
light-vessel with that tack, so we stood o
it, then went about again, and fairly surge(
that white occulting light, which had be
it were a personal possession.

I suppose it was near eleven o'clock w
question of the colour of Aransgrund's
finally settled.   At midnight we were
cable's length of it, rushing through t
without sidelights, dependent as usual u
riding light which I carried in the well.   I h;
to go into Helsingfors by daylight, for I
know the channel and, more important, 1
did not know the way to the Nylands Yac

I therefore decided to take a pilot, and, havi
no flares, waved the riding light. For a long tir
there was no reply, when, thinking that perha
he took our riding light for the ordinary white lig
carried on the open fishing-boats, we hooted
him with the fog-horn. This may have be
extremely incorrect, but it had an instantaneo
result. Figures moved on the light-vessel's deck
We heard shouts, and presently someone beg:
swinging a lantern round in circles. They h:
understood, and all we had to do was to ke
Racundra near the light-vessel while they launch
a boat and put the pilot on board. This was n
so easy as it might seem. Remembering tl
experience of Baltic Port, we had feared to ta
sail off her in spite of the wind, and, hove to, sl
was knocked about considerably, and drifted t
near the vessel or else slipped off into the out
darkness. All this was probably due to our la
of knowledge of her. On later occasions I had h
hove to under full canvas in the most decoro
and ladylike manner. Anyhow, there was o
horrid moment when we thought we were comi
into violent contact with the light-vessel, the gre
bulk of which was heaving up and down in a mo
portentous manner right above us. The busine
of getting their boat out seemed very long, and v
learnt afterwards that the pilot had been in h
bunk and had to get up and dress.

" Who are you ? " they shouted at us.

" English yacht," we yelled back, and after tha

in the water, a bobbing lantern appeari
disappearing in the waves, a bump, and
Finnish pilot tumbled on board with : "
do you want to go ? . . . Nylands Club
Right. Keep Grohara light so. Now, Captai
And with that, as pilots do, he expressed
and thirst.

I fed him and poured Riga vodka int
while he asked me, " Did we not see y
as night fell, close by a three-masted schoo
" You did."

He laughed. " Do you know, we report
by wireless to Helsingfors as a likely si
and told them to look out for you ! You
the very last boat we thought would need a

I suspect that the reason why they ha
so long in answering our signals from the li
was that they supposed that, being sm
we were playing some new trick on them
Esthonian smugglers, of whom there are
make it their sport to tease the Finnish
guards. I had heard much about it on th
side of the Gulf, where the smugglers are, a
times in England, the heroes of the lo
population. One man in particular makes
boast that he gets his cargo into Finlan
different method every time, and each tim
care to let the coastguards know the wa
have been tricked. On one occasion he
at evening with a cargo of spirits covered

officers while it was still dark and in a great ﹖
of perturbation asked them what he was to
as in clearing up on deck he had acciden
broken their seals. " Fined two hundred m
for breaking the official seals." He paid the
Then, when he left, he sent a small keg of sp
to the Customs officers, with a note expres
his gratitude for having been allowed for so s
a sum to bring in such and such a quantit
spirit. After many such exploits he was actu
caught and imprisoned, and it was announce
the newspaper that he had been captured
fifteen hundred litres of spirit. He wrote ir
nantly to the editor to say that he had
captured with three thousand litres of spirit,
fifteen hundred, and wanted to know what
become of the rest. The Censor, he complai
did not allow his letter to be published.

When the pilot had finished his meat and d
we went on deck again, where Wirgo, recov
from his illness, was steering. I had left
matches on the cabin table and went down a
to get them. Responsibility gone, the pilo
charge, and *Racundra* already safely acros
thought I would lie down for a moment.
of the last thirty-two hours I had been twe
eight in the steering-well. I lay down, jus
I was, the box of matches in my hand; and t
hours later, matches still in hand, rushed on de
a panic, to find lights all about us, smooth w

me to drink more vodka and collect hi
paid the money and uncorked bottles h
and wholly angry. Twenty-eight hours of
in calm and fog, and then to sleep like a lo
this last three hours of good sailing weat
when I had meant to use the pilot in order
for myself how not to need him again !

NEXT morning I came on deck to find *Racu*
in the delightful anchorage of the Nylands Y;
Club. The Club House is itself on an island,

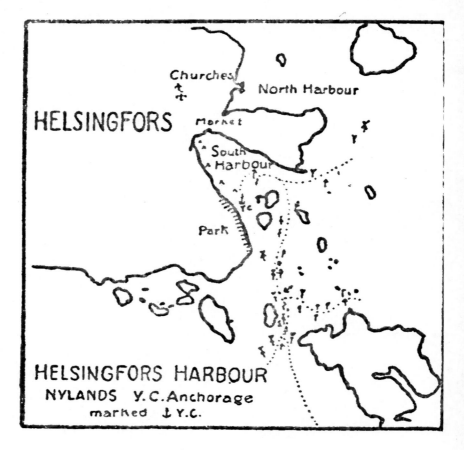

HELSINGFORS

Churches
North Harbour

Market

South
Harbour

Park

HELSINGFORS HARBOUR
NYLANDS Y.C.Anchorage
marked ↓Y.C.

buoys in this southern corner of He
harbour.   The harbour proper lay before
white steamships along the quays, on whi
the low Customs houses, the booths of
market, blue trams slipping swiftly by—
comfortable scene—while over all were tl
domed church and the cathedral spires
have often admired from the sea when
bigger but not better than *Racundra*.   Wi
I went ashore in the dinghy, he to hur
to Reval by steamship and I to look for th
who, after waiting for us last night in t
House, had supposed that the fog had ke]
the other side of the Gulf.

In comparison with Riga and Reval, He
seemed not to have suffered from the wa
shops were full of all the things which for
few years most Baltic towns have had to
out.   With its clean white steamers ai
trams, it seemed more Swedish than
Finland, real Finland, is to be found in the
not in the capital; and walking through th
of this modern Western town, with its rest
and taxi-cabs, I kept thinking of the simple
life I had tasted in Finland years ago
Hittola, by Lake Ladoga, paddling with
in a canoe-shaped boat, I remember fi
little ancient steam-yacht lying covered in
reedy bank of a river.   I was told that in
it had made a voyage to Edinburgh an
It was dropping into decay, that aged little s

"RACUNDRA" AT HELSINGFORS (AFTER SWINGING THE S

of the Arctic, had seen similar strange thi
Looking north from that place to the Pole
nothing but wild country, lake, marshes, rag
forest and ice-infested seas. The little ste
yacht did not seem more foreign to it than
trim stone-built capital.

So far as *Racundra* was concerned, I wasted
that day in friendship. But early next morr
there was a coughing and spluttering and spit
alongside, and I tumbled out to find that by t
friendship *Racundra* was to profit after
Commander Boyce had brought his little mo
boat, *Zingla*, to take me for a run round the hark
to show me the way through the buoys and
into the fairway, which I had missed by falling as
as we were coming in. We ran out one way
ran in another through well-marked chan
between the uncompromising rocks. The Finr
coast is not a coast on which to make mista
and I was glad I had not attempted the foolishr
of trying to find the Club for the first time in
dark. Once you know where it is, however
is easy enough. There are short cuts for sr
boats, but any yacht coming in here for the f
time can do so safely by following the sai
directions for big ships until she is well into
southern harbour. Once there, she has but to fol
the quay round into the southern corner of t
harbour and, if she cannot find a spare buoy, d
anchor until morning.

After introducing me to a score or so of sr

time—indeed, for the only time on the whol
except for getting water—made up his mind
ashore. He wanted a special size of sail
needles, besides some scrubbing brushes an
which he did not trust me to buy. He wa:
the least interested in the town. " Town;
he, " are all one and all dirt." This was a r
libel on the spotless Helsingfors, but the
had been a little embittered by the thick f
black grease which our waterline had a
while lying in the harbour of Reval.

We spent an exciting and expensive n
We bought new brass rowlocks for the
which the builder had disfigured with coars
galvanised iron rubbish which chafed th
and did not fit. We bought rope fende:
bought every block we could find that w
our ropes, and regretted that we had not
buy them the day before, for we could o;
half a dozen and could not wait while th
sent to Abo for more. We bought mops,
and stiff. We bought needles, shackles,
for the staysail, hooks for a hoisting strop
dinghy, a vast hook with a strong spring
picking up a mooring buoy, a tin of colza
the binnacle, brass clips for the main and
peak halyards, besides bread, butter, cheese,
Swedish oatcake, tobacco, stocking-caps,
Finnish sheath-knife, a gorgeous piratica
with a horse's head for a hilt, a handl

signalled to the Club boatman and were put
board our ship.

Then I went ashore again to inquire abou
compass-adjuster, for I had seen a steamship b
slowly shifted round and round a big woo
dolphin close astern of us. I had seen the w
painted marks on the cliff and on buildings,
that I had no doubt as to what was being d
I was anxious to get our own compass corre
and a table of deviations drawn up, so that
homeward voyage might be made with a sm:
proportion of guess-work. The Ancient, as alw
was for starting at once.

" The compass is right enough," said he. "
found the way here with it and you'll find the
back."

I showed him the list I had made of obser
inexactitudes, some of them as much as two ar
half points (for the compass was immediately (
the motor), but he was unconvinced, and I
him hauling up the sails, " to dry," as he s
but really, as I well knew, in hopes that, se
them up, I should myself be persuaded 1
Helsingfors had done enough for us and 1
we might put to sea. When I came back from
harbour office he had already fixed the hook
strop on the fore-halyard and was prepared to 1
the dinghy on board. He said nothing, but co
not hide his disappointment when I told him t
at eight o'clock next morning we were to be

back from racing at Cowes, and looking
slim body, built for speed and nothing el
then over the water to the stout, impert
Racundra, I thought how differently men ta
pleasures on the sea.   I would not have h
gift, and I am sure that Mr. Donner, her
would turn in disgust from my comfortable
After dinner I went into the Club library an
there a really wonderful collection of sailin
from all the countries of the world.   I re
again that excellent little book by Thomas :
Day, the American ; and then, for the fir:
settled down to read McMullen.   Few be
sailing fail to quote McMullen, but his ov
is rare, and I was glad enough to read, o:
on a Finnish island, the story of *Orion's*
from France and of McMullen's enviable
sitting in the cockpit of *Perseus*, the tille
his arm, in mid-channel on a starlit ni;
observed that McMullen, even in our te:
climate, laid up his ships early in Septemb
looking at the calendar, remembered t
were far from home.   It was after midnigh
I put the book back on its shelf and, droppi
the pierhead into the dinghy, threaded :
in the dark through the little fleet to *Ra*
gleaming portholes, for the Ancient, long
had thoughtfully lit the cabin lamp.

recording the event, and, if you are not such
they, you are left wondering how they did
At least, that was so with me. I was left wonder
and was ashamed to ask. But the business
ship-swinging is an interesting one, and whe
experienced mariners may skip the next few p:
graphs, I am sure there must be inexperien
mariners, and even people who are not marii
at all, who will be glad to know how the thin
done and, in place of the cabalistic words " sw
the ship," to have an actual picture of the s
being swung, or rather being lugged by main fc
round a wooden dolphin until she headed in turr
each one of the thirty-two points of the comp

There was a hard N.E. wind blowing in
morning, and letting ourselves swing by a long
from the mooring buoy to which we had made f
we paid out line slowly as we worked stern 1
towards the dolphin, the anchor hanging deer
the water ready to hold us up. When near
dolphin, we loosed the buoy and held v
the anchor while I got into the dinghy and too
warp across to the dolphin. Then we hauled
the anchor, and, shortening the warp, were swing
close by the dolphin while waiting for the arri
of the stout, red-faced, English-speaking Finn v
spent every day of his life in the swinging of
ships.

The dolphin is a stout wooden erection, b
of piles and so fixed in the bottom of the s

walk. Round the upper cone is an ir
working in a groove. At opposite sides
belt are rings, and from these rings warps a:
to the bow and stern of the ship.   The ship
against the lower cone and, in whatever c
it may point, is kept in position by the v
the revolving ring. A steamship is sw
simply steaming round the dolphin and in
with it, stopping for a moment at each ⟨
point.

The principle of the thing is simple
The dolphin may be taken as a fixed poi
the land, at a considerable distance from
marks so placed that when the ship is in
with the dolphin and heading directly on
these marks, it is heading towards a know
of the compass. By observing at this mon
compass to be corrected, it is easy to ⟨
exactly what its error is on that particulaɪ

Just as we were making fast a small b
rowed out to us carrying the red-faced Fiɪ
was a little disconcerted to find that the
was to swing was so very much smaller t
big vessels to which he was accustomed.
ever, he paid her a compliment or two ᴠ
heard where she had come from, and s
seriously about his business, after hurt:
feelings a little by asking :

" Will I put my foot through if I stand
cabin roof ? "

heavy tripod carrying a sighting apparatus.
his command we pulled *Racundra* round t
dolphin till he had one of the marks in line v
his instrument. The dolphin was built for
swinging of big ships, and we had trouble in adjust
things so that we could use it for *Racundra*. '
edge of the platform pressed against our shro
and we had to take them down on one side.
decorated her side with all our fenders, and find
them insufficient, used our spare mattresses. H
ever, in the end we got the thing to work. '
Finn would call out the actual bearing,
N. by W., or whatever it was, while I, darting
our steering compass, called out the bear
indicated by the card and the lubberline.
had in no way exaggerated the inaccuracies. '
Finn had brought with him two magnets brigh
painted, which he screwed down in the steeri
well in positions found by experiment. Th
magnets roughly compensated for the effects
the mass of iron in the motor, so that the comp
became more or less correct. Then, point by poi
with the help of a couple of sailors borrowed fr
another yacht, we pulled *Racundra* round and h
her steady on each one of the thirty-two poir
noting at each point the difference between act
and compass bearing. It took a long time, for
wind was strong, *Racundra* heavy and the F
conscientious. However, it was done at last, a
down in the cabin, over a bottle of vodka

steer by our compass. By noon the w‹
done. I put the Finn ashore and hung
completed table in the cabin.

With that we were both for starting w
wind held, late in the day though it was.
in water, made my farewells at the Nylan
and, without anchoring again, cast off
from the dolphin and tacked out of the h

HELSINGFORS TO REVAL

IT was 1.15 when we sailed, with the barome
at 30.1 and rising and the wind strong a
easterly. The Nylands Club had been racing
the morning, and we met many of their bo:
coming in heavily reefed as we worked out throu
the buoyed channel which Boyce had shown
the day before. Three big grey ships of t
British Fleet were at anchor in the outer harbo
but we were having our work cut out for us, twisti
in and out among the buoys, and had small ti:
to look at them. Outside there was a steep
sea, and we were getting a little splashed ev
before reaching Grohara island, which we pass
at 2.20.

Grohara is a small rock with a stout wh
lighthouse upon it, to be left to westwards. T
last time I had passed it in daylight was in wint
time, when an icebreaker was ploughing a w
through the ice for a convoy of six vessels, a
then there was the wreck of a little steamer tl
had tried to pass Grohara on the wrong side, al
for her error, was held there hard and fast on t
rocks and was covered, hull, masts and riggii

pendulums. It was difficult to believe
jolly little island at which we were lookin
had been, only seven months before, th
of that desolate scene. Now, instead of
hummock in a snow-covered icefield, it
in blue sea, splashed with white, the c
the Finnish flag, while far to north of it
see the little islands and rose-coloured ro
farther yet, on the pale skyline, the do
spires of Helsingfors, a picture only less
in its way than the romantic entr
Stockholm.

From Grohara we steered S. and $\frac{1}{2}$ W.,
rather more for drift than we shou
done, and when we sighted the Ar
light-vessel, found it well away on the s
bow. We steered to pass it close to, w
did at 4.7 (fifteen miles out from Hel
By this time the swell was such that, th
were so near that on the top of a wave
see the caps of the men on the light-vessel
in the trough we could not see the vess
not even the tops of her masts. The w
been blowing hard easterly for most of
we had been in Helsingfors, which was e
account for the size of the waves. We
a little water, and the Ancient, obstinate
put on his oilskins too late, and remarke
" I am already wet in mine starn." I

HELSINGFORS TO REVAL

The wind had shifted a little, but our cou:
gave us a point or two to spare, and we glac
took up the centreboard. Then in a hardish gı
a faulty fastening in the mizen peak halyaı
came adrift and the peak fell down. We lower
the sail and tied it, lashing the boom to the riggi
to prevent its banging about, and found th
sailing as we were, not absolutely closehauled, s
steered perfectly without the mizen. We sail
her so the whole way across the Gulf, the wi
being so lusty that we willingly accepted from
own strength this shortening of sail that we shou
perhaps have been too proud (or too lazy) to rı
in for ourselves.

After this, which happened close by Aransgruı
Racundra settled down to her work and ga
us a most exhilarating sail. It was a gloric
day, bright hard sunshine, with cold in the a
as we get it in the Baltic at the back end of t
year, a good wind heeling her over to the railiı
stiff as she is, and that mighty swell lifting
sky-high and dropping us again into a blue dep
walled by water. It was easy work steering, nı
that the mizen was gone, and we took it in lo:
spells without the least fatigue. "This is bett
than coming across," said the Ancient Marinı
"Wind's all right, but it's fog as I can't stan
There's nothing worse for sailormen than wh
that fog he spreads himself on the water and ı
go howling around all blind."

By nine o'clock we were between Wulf is
Nargon, and could consider that we had
the Gulf.   But we were very far from get
harbour.   The wind had been falling away
evening and shifting to the south, and it
as long to make the ten miles remaining
taken us to cover the thirty-five that we
astern.   Yet   at   this   moment,   before
wholly darkened, we could actually see t
and chimneys of Reval, and the huge
the west of the town, looking like a giga
with outstretched wings.

Then came complete darkness and a
night.   We took turns at the wheel, tl
below occupying itself with the sidelights
say at once that the watch below envied t
on deck, and, cold as it was, preferred th
the sidelights.   Fine copper sidelights tl
too,   pre-war,   bought   last   year   and
expensive.   I had hesitated over the
shocking cost, but had remembered, " Th
the ship, the more her need for good ligl
gone without new shoes, refrained from
new hat, and plumped for the best a
expensive sidelights I could buy.

All winter they had lain in my roo
compass and lead-line, log, sea-anchor,
and cabin lamp, and, shining there v
promise of the summer's cruise, had wa
with an inward glow what time the sl

enough; and it had been a pleasure, steering throu
the quiet night, to know that the green eye a
the red were gleaming brightly for any other sl
to see. But during the gale that followed th
had failed us. We had done our hopeless beati
under jib and mizen, trying to make Baltic Po
with our lights out. We had wallowed about
the night between Pakerort and Nargon knowi
that we showed no light to any other ship. Aga
going into Helsingfors, as the wind got up
Aransgrund, they had failed us, and by now
was abundantly clear that they were but f
weather friends and would burn only in a co
parative calm.

To-night the watch below cleaned them, trimm
them, filled them, brought them on deck and :
them in their places, only to see them go c
abruptly and decisively as soon as they w
there. He took them below, trimmed them aga
wrapped them in sackcloth for shame and
protection, and brought them out again, cuddl
close as if they had been favourite lambs and
a careful shepherd, only to see them drop ir
darkness the moment they felt the wind abc
the cockpit coaming. He devised a new meth
of protecting them, thought of some other w
of keeping them alight, took them below, :
trimmed, relit and brought them up again, nurs
like babies, to receive another blow from F
upon the optimism that grew less sturdy as t

shrinking, tender state as that of the first.
we both gave it up and kept them muffle
galley, hoping to be able at least to sl
dying flash of the right colour to any s]
we might meet.   The riding light, a simpl(
ordinary affair, burned well, and we
among our feet in the cockpit, for warmtl
be able to flourish it in case of urgent ne

We had to beat the whole way into Re
beating is not the thing that we are best
could, however, get along with short legs
ward and then long legs in more or less t
direction.   There was no difficulty al
Reval is a good place to make in the dar
east of the harbour mouth are two lig
standing well back and very high and
almost on the foreshore and low.   The
kept one above the other, lead the whole
until one can see the lights of the harbour (
Moreover, one of them fades and goes
moment the approaching or departing
has strayed to east or west of the safe
So we stood closehauled as near southerl;
could until the light went out, then wer
and sailed on the other tack while it sl
again, came under the high light, slipped
it and again faded and went out, where
tacked once more.   This we repeated con
creeping slowly nearer all the time, growir
and colder as the night wore on.

lights of the men-of-war in the western corner
the bay. We had long lost the muffled mo
and began to rejoice in our slow speed, wh
promised to bring us, as indeed it did, among
crowd of anchored schooners and other sn
vessels in the roads just as the sky was lighten
in the east.

Dimly ahead of us we could see the pale hi
of ships, and already over to the east the dark s
seemed to blench. And then, as it were qu
suddenly, there was more light, and we saw,
if at a signal, the sails of a schooner coming (
of harbour, followed by another and another
the ships that had been waiting for the day
We passed the little steamer lying at anch
tacked through the ships in the roads, crossi
and recrossing the paths of the outgoing schoone
and came to the harbour mouth when in the bl
mist of early morning the red and green lights
either side of the entrance glittered more li
butterflies than lamps. They went out just
we turned in, took off our staysail and round
up to one of the buoys off the Yacht Club mo
We tied the damp sails till we could dry them
the sun, and while the Ancient cleared up
deck, I went below and, with fingers so cold th
I could hardly strike a match, lit the Primus a
boiled water. With that we drank the last of o
English rum, and now, suddenly, too tired to ta
dropped each on his bunk and slept.

REVAL TO BALTIC PORT

SEPTEMBER 5TH, 6.20 a.m. Baromete:
We wasted a day in getting provisions an
on board the fine new gratings for the
the steering-well and the new iron horse
mainsheet, which we stowed in the forec
use next year, as its mass of iron wou
played all sorts of tricks with our newly
compass. The wind that would have se
so well, had we been able to start befe
died away and was replaced early this mo:
a slight breath from the S.E., with w
drifted out of harbour on a clear mornii
the smoke of the Reval chimneys was of
opinions as to what wind was blowing or
any wind was blowing at all. We, howe
made up our minds that the wind was S.E.
the balloon jib as a spinnaker, and wer
to find that it agreed with us and dr
nine o'clock we had brought Karlo island
An hour later we had cleared it and were
to pass close by Surop, the balloon now
staysail.

Changes of sails were always a deligh

IN BALTIC PORT

critically at our balloon, " was in the *Demo*
(*Thermopylæ*). There was she and the *Kutu*
(*Cutty Sark*), and I was in the *Demooply*.
those days there was racing between those sh
and not a man in any ship but would have his
on one or other, if it was only a pound of toba
Double crews they had, and when I first sa
with the *Demooply* I thought officers and n
were all mad. We never left those ships al
We were shifting one sail or another sail for ev
little change of wind. Double crews, but n
too many for the work, and before I had b
on board a week, I was as mad as all the r
There was real sailing done in those days."

To-day, however, no ingenuities in setting can
would have been of any use to us. There ens
a period of absolute calm, accompanied by
psychological storm, for the Cook demanded t
the motor should be used. The Ancient an
have never been shipmates with a motor bef
and we do not like them, trust them or underst
them. After long opposition, and trying to pr
that we were really moving, although the wa
was like glass, we did at last try to wind it
and found that it would not go ; whereupon
Cook asked that it should be thrown overboa
and was not pacified on being told that it
valuable as ballast. However, when a breath
wind came diffidently down to us from the
and we got steerage way again, she relented
gave us luncheon on deck. At 3.30 we had Su

German schooner which had followed us
Reval, away to N. of us by Nargon, with a
sails and spanker set, a fine sight, but too fa
for the camera. By six o'clock we wei
moving through the water N. of Fall, and
already clear that the spell which lies on m
going westward along this strip of coast w
to be broken.

Every time I have sailed from Reval to
Bay or to Baltic Port, I have been becalr
Surop and spent the night drifting betweei
and Pakerort. I have spent as many as
hours on this passage of a score of sea-mil
I face it always with desperate resignation
was to be my record quick passage. Ra
easily beat both Slug and Kittiwake, fc
first of my ships, covered those magic so
miles in under the twenty-four hours. Th
is not laid on that passage going the othe
but you will remember that it was pi
between Pakerort and Surop that we had to
that wild night after our futile attempt t
into Baltic Port with a broken wing.

This night was to be the completest cont
that night of storm. In scarcely rippled
across broad patches smooth as oil, we
slowly towards Pakerort. There was a fiery
over the sea to the N.W., against which th
of the little fishing-boats on the bank o
promontory were as if picked out with

REVAL TO BALTIC PORT

Lahepe Bay on the nearer side of Pakerort. Bl
silhouettes against that fiery sky, they turn
suddenly into pale blots moving against the dar
mass of the cliff. And then the cliff itself fad
and the lighthouse above it shone out, and th
were stars and a wind that you could feel on
back of your hand, but would not blow a mat
flame crooked. The Cook, extremely angry w
the motor, and with us for our philosophic, ind
almost relieved, acceptance of the fact that
smelly little creature would not work, went
bed. The Ancient and I smoked together in
steering-well, after lighting our sidelights, wh
on this calm bright night burned magnificen
We rounded Pakerort and then were met by
very slight breath from the S.E., against wh
we beat slowly into Roogowik.

At anchor, off the harbour, was a ship of
Esthonian Navy. Signal lights were chatter
between her and the harbour. Small boats w
lanterns passed to and fro. The faint wind brou
us the noise of music on board. And then, as
came nearer, someone on board must have noti
us, and we were presently drenched with
blinding cold glare of a searchlight. " They th
we're another little ship-of-war," said the Anci
" and they're afraid we're going to ram them."
not, it was with very bad manners that they k
us in such a glare that we could hardly see what
were doing and could not see the tiny light

then, keeping it so, tacked towards it, a
1.30 a.m., rounded into the harbour.

We found not the comfortable harbour
known before, but one of, temporarily
that size. Two big schooners were lying l
side by side against the outer mole, and v
to tie up to the new tarred quay which
off the anchorage, now dry land, where, witl
happy little boats, *Kittiwake* had her m
last year. We were glad of the new fendei
Helsingfors, and, getting ourselves pretty
managed to keep *Racundra* clean. We t
fore and aft, had a tot of hot but inferic
and went to bed.

OLD BALTIC PORT AND NEW

I FIRST found Baltic Port in *Kittiwake*, a
having found it, made it our headquarters fo
happy summer of minor exploration. I had he:
of it as the Russian Naval Port, and imagined
a kind of Sheerness, busy with motor launch
steam pinnaces and other forms of naval activi
I found it a sleepy little old-time harbour, m:
by moles from the shore enclosing a square ba:
the shore being left as it always had been, so t!
the fishing-boats used to beach themselves uj
it at full speed, a man jumping on the thw
and swinging backward from the shrouds to s:
the mast at the moment of grounding, when tl
often ran a boat half out of the water. The (
Kittiwake struggled in, there was a Brit
steamship, a Wilson boat, the *Cato*, in
harbour, and though she is a small ship, she :
very little room for anything else. I think
Cato called twice that summer, but all the 1
of the traffic there was made up of local schoon(
and the harbourmaster had little else to do !
to sail a smart little skiff to the bank off Paker

watched the crew of the *Cato* beaten at :
by a local team.   Eleven played on each si
the *Cato's* crew had no spare men, v
every man in the Port was waiting round t
to take his turn in the local team, and as on
another took his place.   On another th
lowered away a lifeboat, and we went off
fishing grounds under a standing lug.   At c
of the harbour was a low stage beside v
grey Government launch was moored, end
with a converted fishing-boat, partly tarr
partly painted blue, in which, on Sunday;
visitors were transported to the Roogö
and back.   Once a week the three or four
the Government launch took her out to
mysterious business.   But for the most pa
lay half naked on the stones on the far
the mole or had splashing matches wit:
other.

The little town had much the same chi
Small boys played *gorodki* (a very exciting l
form of skittles) on the broad streets tha
nearly all grass.   Cattle grazed there.
three sheep coming out of church with the
manner of respectable parishioners.   I w
a hare playing by the railway station, where
part of the population used to meet in the ev
to see the train come in from Reval.   The
a post office, and I think three or perhap
four shops.   There was also a fire brigad

the town was very much interested and ask
them how much they got. There could not
a pleasanter little place.

But with growing traffic in the Baltic, su
quiet could hardly continue in a port which in
but the most exceptional winters is free from i(
There are fifteen fathoms of water between t
mainland and Roogö, and the water is deep almc
to the shores. Long after the way into Reval
blocked with ice, ships can come freely in
Roogowik and into Baltic Port itself. Peter t
Great and Catherine after him realised what cou
be done with such natural advantages, and reli
of their work show what Baltic Port may y
become. Just north of the harbour is the old fo
carved out of the cliff itself, with deep moa
which must once have been sunk to sea-level,
very near it. There are the old bastions, cunning
laid out as in Peter's project, the old gun-positioi
with sheer cliff below them on the side facing t
bay, and on all other sides cliffs also, invisil
from a yard or two away, made by cutting t
moat down from the high land—a moat a hundr
yards across, winding this way and that all rou
the fort, with perpendicular sides of solid ro(
The work was done with convict labour and t
labour of prisoners of war, and all this stuff (
out of the rock was tipped into the sea to ma
the mole that he had planned to stretch acr(
the bay and to turn it into the finest enclos

on the other side, where you can still see
natural line of the coast is broken, the
building another fort and a second mole
the first.   On that side they did not get
but on this the spar-buoy north-west of the
marks the end not of a natural reef but o
artificial causeway and breakwater, wh
finished as it is, serves to protect the st
beach   always   covered   with   fishing-bo
drying nets between the fort and the
When I was there there were wild roses
in the fort.   Columbines and Canterbu
were growing in the moat, and, lying up
the top of the old gun-positions, I used t
hot afternoons looking out to sea, thin
Peter and his passion for ships, and eating
strawberries.

On the shingle below the fort, where the
sit, with their children, fastening small fla
as sinkers to the bottoms of the nets,
German mine being put to a purpose
opposite to that for which it was intende
fishermen were building a new boat.   Her
laid and they were putting on the planking
were busy steaming the planks, and the
was a German mine, emptied of its ex
and neatly fixed over a small furnace o
from the beach.   How they had managec
the explosives out I do not know, but h
the mine with a good fire under it, boilir

with coffee that day when I first came in the
so tired that I fell asleep with my head on the tal
before ever I could put the coffee to my li
With him I used to sail in his little skiff, whi
he could steer by merely shifting his own hu
weight forward or aft. With her I used
remember my own North country, where also t
good wives will tell you what a fool you
at the very moment when they are drying yc
boots and mixing you a hot grog to save you fro
the cold that you have earned. I met her o
day going to Reval with great bundles of lil
blossom under her arm for a friend in town, a
on her head, instead of the pretty green sha
she wore at home, a hat with an enormous wh
ostrich feather, exactly in the front of it, wavi
like a helmet plume. She had had this feather 1
nineteen years, she said, had never washed it, h
never gone into Reval without it, and yet it w
still as white as when it was new. It had surviv
many hats. Nineteen years before, her husbar
a sailor then, came back from a voyage. S
had forgotten where he had been, but no matte
he came back in a hard winter, when even Bal
Port was frozen in, and he left his ship stuck
the ice and came home to her to Pakerort Ligl
house on Christmas Eve, across the frozen se:
with two ostrich feathers, this and another, betwe
his shirt and his skin, so escaping the Custoi
officers. "And were you pleased with him?"

but a ha'porth of sense he'd have brou
white one and one black."

What with talks with the harbourma
his wife, whose roughness of tongue wa
defence for the softness of her kind hea
the lighthouse-keeper from Odensholm, v
to sail in now and again in a little ha
sloop, and with the skippers and crews of
sailing vessels which, but for the Cat
all the traffic of the harbour; what w
fishing on the river six miles away, w
took Kittiwake's dinghy on a country c
days in wind and sunshine on Peter's fort
cliff by Pakerort, I liked Baltic Port we
times, but perhaps best of all in the c
after sundown, when we used to sit on K
green cabin roof, there being no other c
after the swilling of the decks.   The old w
would carefully lay his long pipe on th
outside his wooden hut, and wander slow
the harbour to climb the rickety iron lac
light the light at the harbour mouth.   V
were there, in May and June, it was nev
dark.   A guitar would tune up in one
schooners, an accordion in another.   Mos
little ships carried family parties, skipp
and little skipperlets, and there would be
on the decks, while the local beauties v
back in the stern-sheets of the dinghy l
to the Government launch and be rowe

the landbreeze that comes with the setting
the sun.

Now all is changed. There, where *Kittiwa*
lay to her anchor, is now the new quay, on whi
they say there is to be a railway and a crar
Things may be better when the works in progre
are finished, for new moles are to be built ai
the harbour will be twice the size. Things w
be better for the big ships busy on the Russi:
trade, but I doubt if they will be better for us. T.
harbourmaster is too busy to sail his little ski
The few shops have already multiplied to a doz
or more, and whereas, in the old days, the harbou
master's wife was only sometimes willing to gi
lodging to those whom she counted her frien(
there is now a regular hotel, the rooms of whi
are full of busy, serious people, interested in t
new activity of the port. Big steamers with st(
cables will soon leave no room for the schoone
and little ships like *Racundra* and *Kittiwake* w
never again find Baltic Port the delightful la
anchorage that it was a year ago.

THE ROOGÖ ISLANDS

WE did not call at Roogö in *Racundra*
were hurrying to get southwards to the p
had not yet visited. But the year b
Kittiwake, we had sailed round betw
two islands, and had landed at the jetty
can see from the quay at Baltic Port and
all over Little Roogö. The inhabitants
islands, men, women and even pigs, are
Swedes. When I first rounded up ther
aged men and a pig strolled out on the
inspect us, and began at once by asking
spoke Swedish. I told them in Swedish
did not, or only very little, but they w
suaded that I was only teasing them, ai
at last they were convinced they lost all
and strolled disappointed away. The pig i
on guard, and when I landed, resented my j
worrying round me like a good housedog
sure that if I had been a Swede he wou
wagged his tail and licked my hand.

A day or two later, however, Leslie jo
from Reval, and we crossed to the islan
He had lived in Christiania and Copenha

appointed by not being a Swede. But Les
went boldly up past the little windmill to the fi
of the wooden cottages to buy eggs. He return
discomfited with the news that this cottage w
inhabited exclusively by widows who did not ke
hens. I had gone farther and found anotl
cottage outside which some sort of Sunday parl
ment was in progress, half a dozen men and t·
or three women sitting on logs and stools, the m
smoking long pipes. Spurred by competition
a linguist with Leslie, I shouted out boldly, " H
ni naugra egg ? " with electrical effect. A wom
with a white shawl over her head leapt up a
disappeared on the run towards some outhous
The gathering broke up. Everyone slipped aw
and ostentatiously busied himself or herself wi
something or other, and when Leslie and the Co
came up they refused to believe that I had do
anything but terrify the population. Gradua
the men and women, having as it were put the:
selves in the right by being found busy, desert
their imaginary occupations and came half-hearteo
towards us. In the background I could see t
fleet runner in the white shawl and green petticc
darting from outhouse to outhouse with a bask
An old humpbacked witch, certainly not over fo
and a half feet high, with a bright maroon sh
hanging loose outside her petticoat, hobbled fro
a cottage to stare at us from afar, and present
the egg-gatherer, shielded by a group of frien∢

come from ?   How long had we been
Port ?   My Swedish, having obtained e{
away behind Leslie's Scandinavian flue
bought butter, but had no paper to {
The old man who sold it us said at onc
could take their saucer and bring it ba
evening when we had done with it, a r(
proof of the honesty of the islanders
consequent belief in the honesty of o
Russia such a loan would have been un
On the mainland here, the canny len(
have asked for a deposit of at least twice
of the saucer.   We settled the matter k
the butter in the biggest of our tin mu{

  We walked out of this village of
together with three mottled cows, dri
woman with a handkerchief on her he{
orange and white, a deep rich green sk
bodice of bright purple, flaming like a
we walked we were joined by other w
other cows, until at last there was a co
herd, driven by four women with long s
an open space of moorland, green grass a{
with grey rocks showing through the tu
on either hand were enclosed with s{
built without mortar, like our walls in }
and Westmorland, but lower, because
are round, sea-worn boulders and har(
together than the flat slates at home.
we broke away from our companions

pinewoods of the mainland, but birchwoods, an
under their silver stems, wherever the ground wa
not a morass, were lilies of the valley. Near th
far edge of the woods we stopped and cooke
our dinner under the shadow of a great rock on
good fire of birch, which is the best of all tree
for the heat that is in it. Climbing to the top (
the rock and standing upon it, I could just se
the glint of water, and beyond it the dark wood
of the other or Greater Roogö.

After dinner, a pipe and some flower-gatherin;
we went slowly out of the woods and across on
stone wall after another until we came down o
the western shore of the island and found a scene (
astonishing strange beauty. The shore, flat, wit
scattered boulders, seemed to slip unwillingly int
the sea. The water, dotted with rocks, so that :
looked as if one could walk ankle-deep from on
island to the other, was quite smooth. And i
the middle of this shining water, a quarter of
mile away, was a green islet, with a little wood a
its southern end, and behind this wood, her bow
and tilted bowsprit showing and her tall mast
heeling over above the trees, was a black two
masted sailing ship, aground. Beyond were th
bluer waters of the bay, ruffled with wind ; beyon
them again the wooded shore of the mainland.]
might have been the opening scene of a boy'
story of a pirate island. Nor did the scene los
any of its romantic character as we came neare
and saw the black tarred ship reflected in shallo\

she got there I could not say, nor how she]
to depart thence.   The waters of the Balti
along these shores when the wind is fron
and W., but I did not think that they c
so high as to float this vessel, which, und
her anchor out as if in deep water, her m
rigging intact and fretting the sky, seeme
ladder, with a gesture of renunciation,
given up the sea for good and made the
resting place for ever.

We walked on southwards along th
looking at the windmills, which are m
small, like large dovecots, to the village of
which, though called the lesser, is really t
of the two on the island.   It is a fishing
and on the shore close by are many little
harbours, each big enough for one or at n
small open boats.   At the head of each
little shallow landing places is a shed, h
the nets and other instruments.   There w
nets on hoops, with wide wings opening fr
mouths, for the catching of pike, and t
very fine nets, like gossamer, some of then
a faint blue, for catching the little silv
which, salted or preserved in oil, are a :
Esthonian diet.   Then there were the b
the nets—wooden buoys, each one carved
its owner would know it ; buoys shaped lil
bells, balls, crosses, with flags and witho
lettered and unlettered.

ROOGÖ WINDMILL.

which just then were in full bloom. It seemed
first deserted, but as we turned up towards it fro
the edge of the sea we saw two old men leani
on a gate in conversation. Both of these me
and a younger man who joined them later, we
dressed like sailors, in blue striped jerseys und
their coats. Leslie, as Scandinavian scholar, w
thrust forward as spokesman, and had a gre
success, fully making up for my first failure
the quay at Storaby. It seemed that news of o
arrival had already crossed the island. Th
knew that we were English, and the elder of t
two, evidently the philosopher of the place, tc
us that it was no wonder we could make ourselv
understood, since Swedish, Danish, Norwegia
German and English were all from the same ste
and were the five great languages of the worl
Politely trying to make us feel at home and amo
friends, he asked how we were getting on wi
our coal strike and wanted us to tell him abo
Ireland, which he confounded with Courlan
though when Leslie said that the Courlande
were now independent and called their count
Latvia, he at once explained that he meant
country somewhere that belonged to England.

The inhabitants of Lillaby are very timorous
strangers. Besides the three fishermen, we cou
not get speech of a soul, though we saw sevei
peeping at us through cottage windows as \
passed on through a seemingly deserted villag
We wanted water and saw a girl in an arohe

can at the pump and came away. Afterw:
saw the girl's head, looking after us round a
of the wall.

We did, however, have one other intervi
that was with a pig. We had come on the
thing to a street to be found on the islan
stone walls, with a mud lane between the
barns and painted cottages on either :
wanted to photograph it, but wanted son
in the foreground, and since there w
inhabitants, and I remembered that rather
pig I had met on my first landing, said
" If only there were a pig." At that mon
turned the corner of a barn, and there
very middle of the lane lay a pig indeed.
such a pig as that described in a novel
Goncourts', which slept a sleep that could
due to a heart of gold and a stomach of ir
lay on the edge of a shadow, in the mudd
of road, its forepaws idly crossed, like the
of a gentlewoman resting from her knittin;
(for it was a feminine pig) raised her he:
grunted at us. The ice was broken. I appr
her with affectionate words, camera in
begging her to move a yard, no more, ir
sunshine. She understood me perfectly,
into the sunshine, and took up one pos
another which she judged characteristic
temperament. I asked her to snuffle in th
and she snuffled in the mud. I took off

THE ROOGÖ ISLANDS

not been for Leslie's conversational successes
would have treated me in the manner of her bro
of Storaby), returned sedately to her place, ju
the lengthening shadows, chose the dampest
that had recently been warmed by the sun,
resumed her calm and contemplative attitud
benevolent repose. Unfortunately, every on
the photographs was a failure.

We met no one else on the island, and came
from the village on wide open grass-land, and
that to the woods, where we gathered lilies o
valley, made fire on a stone and tea, which
drank squatting on our heels, which squel
beneath us in the marsh, while a woodpe
shrieked and jeered in the birch-trees overl
Then, as evening fell, we hurried bacl
Kittiwake, made sail again, and returned to
anchorage in Baltic Port.

THE SHIP AND THE MAN

SAILING from Baltic Port, one of a crew
in another man's ship, I came to the far
the Dagorort Peninsula, and there h
experience which I cannot refrain from
in this book, so full it was of the romance o
rarely visited waters.

*　　　*　　　*　　　*　　　*

We had anchored half a mile from the
off the place that is called Ermuiste, which
" the terrible," for it is a place of many
a rocky point open to the widest sweep of the
across the Baltic Sea. We had not dared
nearer, and I was glad we had not, for, as I
ashore in the little boat, I passed many
awash and saw others a foot or two under
There were dark purple clouds rising over
to the N.W., wind was coming, and w
impatient to be off again, to find shelter,
least to put some miles of sea between us ar
notorious coast. But there was still sunli
the rocky shore and on the dark pinewood

where I meant to land. But, looking over
shoulder as I pulled in, bobbing over the w
in my little boat, I could see none of the th
that a pierhead usually promises. There wa
watchman's hut on the pier, no smoke above
trees, no cottages, no loafers, no fishermen, no
of any kind of life. And then, coming near
saw that the pier was in ruins. Much of
planking had gone, great beams were lea
perilously over from it, and here and there ma
of it had actually fallen into the water. I wi
to waste no time, and was on the point of tur
and pulling back to the ship, when I saw somet
else more promising than the pier. Just w:
the forest that stretched down to the be
almost hidden by the tall pines, was the g
golden body of an unfinished ship. Where a
was building, there, surely, must be men, ai
rowed in confidently past the ruined pier, sli]
off my shoes, rolled up my trousers and, jum
overboard, pulled the little boat through sha
water and up on a narrow strip of small peb'

Then, walking up into the shadow of the tre
came to the ship, the upper part of which,
above my head, was glowing in the splashe
sunshine that came through the tops of the p
which brushed the sides of the ship as they we
in the gathering wind. There was not a mai
be seen, or a hut for men, nor was there sc
of hammers or any of the usual accompanim
of shipbuilding. But for the ruined pier and

things about the ship herself which seemed
odd. She was a very large ship to be
on that bit of coast, where there is no real
and the most ambitious launches are thos
twenty-foot fishing-boats which a man
during the winter to earn his living in the
months. She seemed even larger than she
ships do on land, shut in there among t
that pressed about her as if they had gr
round her. And her lines were not those c
ship. There was something a little old-fe
about them, as though she were an un
masterpiece of an older period. A few sc
of her type survive to-day among those "
that carry timber and potatoes round the Es
coast, and they outsail those modern ships i
an obstreperous motor, tucked away in th
makes up for the want of the love and thou
went into the lines of the older vessels. A
I saw that I was wrong in thinking that
been newly planked. The upper planking v
certainly, ruddy gold where the sun caught
lower down her hull was weathered. O
topmost planks had been freshly put on,
the eye descended from them it passed
ceptibly from a new to an old piece of shipk
The keel, laid on great stones, was joined
by moss. There was lichen upon it, and
foot of the stern-post was a large bright
of scarlet toadstools.

the silence and the trees into a small clearing a
a loud noise of grasshoppers. There was a t
hayfield, not bigger than a small suburban gard
a cornfield, perhaps three times the size, and
old log cabin with a deep thatched roof, an o
house or two, a dovecot and pigeons flutter
about it.

The pigeons fluttered and murmured, but
dog barked and no one answered when I knocl
at the low door of the hut. I knocked again, a
then, doubtfully, tried the wooden latch, oper
it and walked in. A very little light came throu
the small windows, heavily overhung by the d
thatch. The hut was divided into two rooms.
the first were a couple of spinning-wheels, one v
old, black with age, the other quite new, a pre
copy of it, the two contrasting like the up
planking and the keel of that still unfinished sl
There was also a narrow wooden bed, a great
chest and a wooden stool, all made as if to l
for ever. A few very clean cooking things w
on the stove and fishing-lines and nets w
hanging from wooden pegs on the walls.
second room held no furniture but a bench an
big handloom for weaving. There was some gr
strong canvas being made upon it, and, as I lool
at it, I guessed suddenly that here were be
made the sails for the ship.

Without knowing why, I hurried out of
cabin into the sunshine. Leaning on the g

have been any age from fifty to a hundre
clothes were of some strong homespun
probably made on the loom where he was
the sails.   The shoes on his bare brown fe
of woven string with soles of thick rope.
his arrival the whole place seemed to have
to life.   He was accompanied by three she
two pigs snuffled in the ground close by.
impassive as his master, lay beside the ga
opening his eyes, as if he had been wake
sleep.

Somehow I could make no apology for
gone into his cottage.   I asked him where
eastwards along the coast and for the
anchorage sheltered from the north-west.
me what I wanted gravely, and with a cur
of taking his words one by one out of a
room and dusting them before use.   I triec
eggs and butter from him, but he said he
eggs and never made more butter than he
I should get some from the forester at Pal
Luidja, near the anchorage.   I asked hin
the pier.   Once upon a time there had been
here and timber traffic ?

" Yes, but that was a long time ago,
people have all gone away."

" Was it then that you began buildi
ship ? "

" Yes ; that was when I began build
ship."

myself oddly hurried as I pushed our little b
into the water and rowed away. I could j
catch the sunlight splashes on the body of
ship among the trees. Would she ever be finishe
And what then? What had he planned as
worked at her year after year? Would he
before his dream came true, or before he knew t
the dreaming was the better part of it?

But the sunlight faded and the wind h
freshened, and for a time I thought no more ab
him, for we had enough to do with our own sl

BALTIC PORT TO SPITHAM

SEPTEMBER 7TH. Barometer 30.25. W
dawn, S.W. slight. We sailed at 7 a.m.
incident, except that in pushing our way ou
the eastern quay the sharp point of o
boathook (a Dvina lumberman's pole with
sharp spike on the end, used for handling
logs) stuck fast in the wooden piles and the
mained quivering there, like the Trojan's s
the wooden sides of that barrack of a horse,
was extracted by a good fellow who climbe
for it and brought it round to the narrow l
mouth and gave it back to us as we i
the pierhead. We then had a fair wind ou
bight into which we had so laboriously tac
night before last. It was a fair wind, but
light one. It shifted to the S., and at 8.20 v
at the mouth of the bay on a line betwe
point of East Roogö and Pakerort.

We bore up to pass as near as might b
Roogö Point, where the English charts ar
in marking " a conspicuous tree." The tr
very little one, but it is the only one c
desolate promontory ; no, not quite the on

be conspicuous in its stead. The tree is de
long live the tree!—and the charts shall need
correction. Would that similar precautions
been taken in other places!

It was a glorious morning of brilliant sunsh
but the wind grew less and less, and what tl
was was shifting against us. At 9.45 we were
West Roogö spar-buoy, close by the wind
heading W.S.W. and ½ W. At eleven we v
still between West Roogö and Grasgrund,
were now on the starboard tack and hea
S.W. and ½ W., the wind having shifted northe
The rock of Grasgrund, which had been vis
on our way eastwards, was now not alone,
a considerable island had appeared above wa
A fishing-boat had tied up to this amphib
place and a couple of lads were sunning themse
on ground far out at sea which is almost alw
a foot or two under water. Far inshore, beł
Roogö island, we sighted a cutter which
probably spent the night by the little villag
Wichterpal, now slowly working westwards
ourselves. We held her all day.

At noon the wind increased a little, con
from W.N.W. We set the mizen staysail and t
to pretend to ourselves that we were moving q
fast. We were able to keep more or less on
course, and, as the afternoon wore on, Odensh
from being a row of spots on the horizon bec
a visible definite island, with a lighthouse at

not lit, and we had no longer the smallest
of getting there by daylight. Once rou
point of Spithamn we should have a long
go for shelter. Looking S. towards the l
saw that the cutter which had sailed abeam
from the Roogö islands was far inshore,
making for the hither side of Spithamn, v
schooner was already at anchor. We made
minds to trust to " local knowledge " and
same. We altered our course, and having tl
free, stood straight in for the two ships, enc
by seeing the cutter round up close by the s
and lower her sails just as we put the he
We sailed in close by the rocky side of Spitha
saw the six windmills (five according to the
but really six) on the little hill. Boats,
gunwale deep in firewood, were coming of
to the schooner, just as I had seen last y
the northern coast of Dagö, where also
harbour. The schooners anchor off shore
wood is carried into the water on little carl
packed into boats, leaving just room for a
of boys, who on reaching the ship throw th
up log by log to the captain, his wife, h
and his children, who stow it in the hold.
wind blows on shore, loading is interrupted a
schooners put to sea, returning when a ch
wind brings smooth water.

As we slipped along towards them, the ·
of the cutter gave us the use of his local kn

captain's hail and wave, instantly obeyed, sa
us by a few yards. When we had cleared the sl
he waved again, and five minutes afterwards
were at anchor beside the others. We were th
—the firewood-loading schooner, big and qu
new, the elderly cutter, about twice our own s
and the little *Racundra*, shielded from the W.
Spithamn Point (Spint Head on English char
more or less shielded from the E. by the dist
islands of Roogö, but open to the N. and N.
with nothing but the little island of Odensh(
between us and the coast of Sweden, near i
hundred miles away. Not a very good anchora
but, as I reasoned, the schooner, being worse tl
ourselves in working to windward, would clear
in plenty of time to give us warning, and
skipper of the cutter would hardly be putting
covers on his sails and be getting ready to
ashore if he had expected anything very i
during the night.

We slung the dinghy overboard with a tac
and the Cook and I went ashore to see w
we could of Spithamn before it grew too d
An elderly man in grey homespuns saw us com
and walked from his cottage just above high-w;
mark down to the shingle. He helped us to i
up the dinghy, and fastened the painter t(
thwart of a boat of his own that was lying i
out of reach of the waves. Then, having in i
manner made us his guests, he spoke to us

pleased to know so many languages, &
that we could answer him a word or two
of them, inquired politely in Swedish
language we preferred to talk, and findi
Russian came easiest to us, went on v
talk in that. He was a Swede and his na
Anders Ringberg. He took the Cook
charge and sold her milk, potatoes, an
very salt fish, which he swore had been
the previous day and were hardly salt
For this gross error, however, he atoned by
her a present of some cranberries and gi
copies of two Swedish newspapers, issued s
for the Swedes of the Esthonian island
relicts of the old Swedish colonisation; th
one a typical local newspaper, with its litt
of gossip about Odensholm, about Runö
Worms, about each one of the Swedish settl
so that no one of its purchasers should fail
in it something of peculiar interest to
It even recorded with proper solemnity t
visits of yachts to the outlying islets.
Ringberg was very disappointed that we co
play the harmonium, for he had one in hi
and had made sure at once that we, as e
people from far countries, would be able
wonderful things with it. Hemp was gro
his garden, and he told us that the n
Spithamn not only build their own boats (tl
built the big schooner that was lying

windmills, of the same form as those on Ro(
island. From the hill I could see down throu
a gap in the pinewoods to the shore on the otl
side of the promontory, where in the trees anotl
schooner was building. Here, so I learnt, there
a better anchorage, but the way into it is extrem
dangerous for those who do not know the roc
There is, of course, no detailed chart of
place.

Coming down the hill again, I walked throu
the village of Spithamn, a village of stout log hu
with, as on Roogö, fine pigs walking about
narrow lanes, and everywhere fishing-nets dryi
Some of the houses were rudely painted w
ochre, but most were the natural colour of
weather-beaten wood, the ends of the logs do
tailed across each other at the corners. (
small hut caught my eye from a long way off w
the word "YORK" upon it in big white lett
I came near to it and found that I was look
at the carved name-board of a ship built into
house. There was the green painted scroll-wc
and in the middle of it, carved deeply from
wood, those big white letters on which, no dou
a many waves had beat before the ship t
carried them went ashore and was broken up,
the profit of the natives, on the rocks beyond
point. An English ship, or may be an Americ
and she must have been wrecked here a long ti
ago, as many others have been wrecked for

been carrying firewood to the schooner (
and grounded. A wire rope was shackle
ring on the waterline under her bows, and
a hand at winding her up over fir rollers by
of a primitive capstan deeply bedded in the
Two small men of Spithamn, aged abou
I suppose, were early beginning their in
career, sailing against each other two b
models of their fathers' broad-bowed sc
They were wading in the water, and one (
brought his model ashore to show me.
detail of the rigging was there, and the h
built like the ships themselves, decked,
hatch amidships, a small square, half-sunl
house aft, the wheel behind that, the sail:
and not high, with large topsails, two jibs
staysail.

The skipper of the cutter had made
trips to the shore and back with things
brought in his ship. He was now unload
little boat for the last time. He had l
ashore sacks of coal for the winter, mucl
gear, and a heavy, iron-bound ancient trur
told me of the harbourage there is in Ode:
and said he always left his cutter there
winter, when ice makes sailing impossible. '
no matter what may be, the ice can nevel
her.'' He himself spends the winter asho:
in Spithamn. He asked if we were not tl
that had come to Reval during the gale

OUR NEIGHBOUR AT SPITHAMN.

heart, as compliments to *Racundra* always
warm it, I made my way back along the sh
to the dinghy, where the Cook had already arriv
with her parcels. We rowed back through smoc
water, for the wind had fallen altogether, so tl
I was glad we were not drifting about on t
other side of the point; and after we had h
supper and decided that Anders Ringberg oug
not to have mistaken his fish for fish caug
yesterday, we smoked in the cockpit and look
towards the village. It was nine o'clock. The
was not a light to be seen. Everyone in the pla
had gone to bed. The blinking light on Roc
showed far away, and the light on Odenshol
and we could just see another behind the tre
on the point warning the " Yorks " of these da
not to come to provide nameboards for t
Spithamn houses. Schooner and cutter were
perfect darkness, so *Racundra* ran her ridi
light up the forestay to serve alike for herself a
her big sisters, and we turned in and slept.

After midnight I went on deck and found t
wind easterly, the moon high, clouds overhe
moving from the S., and the sea nearly calm.

SEPTEMBER 8TH. Barometer 30. We had
night at our Spithamn anchorage. I went
two or three times, but those high clc
midnight had been true prophets; th
changed to the S., *Racundra* swung w
nose to the land, and at dawn the sea was
rippled. Those six windmills on the sk
the hill were now on our starboard bow,
had a kindly little wind to take us out
again and round the point, after which i
be clean in our faces, for I had set m
on going due S. and taking *Racundra*
the channel between Worms and the m
instead of back by the way we had come
the deeper, wider channel between Wor
Dagö. The *Baltic Pilot* says: " Hapsal [
we were bound] can be approached fr
northward by the channel between Worn
Nukke Peninsula, but it is so narrow and
that the navigation is difficult even wi
knowledge, assisted by the buoys." Thei
need to explain to any yachtsman the pa
desire of everyone on board to take *R*

beat S., get into the shelter of the land as n
the channel as we could, and, if the wind shou
change, why, then rejoice and run through
Hapsal.

The wind did not change, and blew from t
S., shifting in its most annoying manner, so th
every time we went about we found oursel
pointing nothing like so well as we had hop
We spent twelve tedious hours in making t
dozen miles between Spithamn and the entrar
to the channel, sailing, of course, a very mu
greater distance as we zigzagged against th
fitful wind. As soon as we rounded Spithamn
about half-past seven in the morning we met thi
schooners racing northwards neck and neck; a
after that throughout the day a long processi
of sailing vessels with their booms wide o
schooners goose-winged, came rejoicing from t
S., whither we were painfully beating. Stur
Wormsö schooners, a few clean, smartly paint
Finns, cutters running home to Reval, othe
bound for Kaspervik, more than twenty sail
counted, and we did not begin to count un
many had already dropped hull-down to nort
ward of us. Ship after ship made a fair   a
unforgivable picture. In a sailing vessel beati
against the wind, meeting other sailing vess
running free, you know the whole bitterness
the poor man picking the crumbs from the flo
at the rich man's feast. And looking at the m

It was smooth-water sailing, and the Co
jam with the cranberries that had been
Ringberg's conscience money in the matt
salt fish. The Ancient was much inter
the jam-making, and, while I was steering
hear them in the galley discussing the 1
valuable art of making marmalade, an art
discovered for ourselves slowly and by 1
accidents, as Charles Lamb's Chinaman le
delights of roast pork through the burnin
house. The recipe for marmalade on 1
is as follows : First buy your oranges ;
your oranges, but do not throw the peel
sea. Then boil the peel. Then—but her
revert to our actual discovery, which w
on *Kittiwake* and not on *Racundra,*
is a far steadier boat. Then (in *K*
make an inadvertent movement from one
the boat to the other and upset the whol
into the bilge. Collect the orange peel 1
bottom boards and stew once more witl
of sugar, when the result will be indisting
from the best English marmalade. The in
discovery, apart from the fact that by this
you can both eat your oranges and ha
marmalade, was the upsetting. Until th
we had not known that the water of
boiling should be poured off, and the final
done with fresh water, and this last is tl
secret of marmalade. Having once disco

got a good fix of our position, with Telness beac
in line on the mainland to the E. of us and S
biness lighthouse far away on the island of Wor
bearing S.W. by W. After that we took tu
in keeping a pretty careful look out, for m
outlying rocks and shoals explain the unwillingn
of the *Baltic Pilot* to give any directions for t
passage except the advice not to try it. By 2
we were about two hundred yards from
Savinova spar-buoy. We went about and, w
a slight change of wind, pointed on the starbo
tack S.E. towards the mainland, going ab
again when we came near the rocks awash north
Telness Point. It had long been clear that
could not hope to get through that day, anc
began to search the chart for a possible anchor
and decided to leave the fairway close to
entrance to the channel and to anchor betw
two shoals north of Ramsholm. Accordingly, af
passing close by the buoys that mark the Sgibne
bank, we steered S.E., keeping the lead goir
and at 6.30, while it was still light enough to
that we had a sandy bottom, let go in two fatho
of water, lowering our sails but not taking
halyards off or putting the covers on, so as to
able to clear out at a moment's notice. Just
we had everything snug, I saw a cutter, the l
of that long procession, coming with a fair wi
from the S. out from between the mainland a
Worms, through the channel I wanted to en

come from the N., we should be able at
get so far in the direction of shelter.

However, the wind did not change, bu
strengthened from the S. We had wa
" to our supper," as we say in Yorkshire,
very snug and quiet in a place rather beas
a sailor's point of view (because it gave us
elbow-room in case of change of wind),
fine to look at. Away to the S.W. was the
island of Worms. S. of us was the desola
of Ramsholm, and far away eastward
low-lying mainland. As dark closed in
there was not a single light to be se
Worms Lighthouse at Saxbiness was at t
side of the island and hidden from us. Oc
had sunk below the horizon to the N. T
no light on shore in cottage or farm. A
tasted all the isolation of Noah's Ark, alo
flood receded and showed the peaks and
of a depopulated earth. She was, however,
upon no Ararat, but swung gently to he
in a little natural harbour, every mole ar
water of which was hidden under water.

RAMSHOLM TO HAPSAL THROUGH TH NUKKE CHANNEL

I HAD left the lead overboard as a means of telli whether our anchor held, and three or four tim in the night I went on deck to have a look at t lead line. Once, when the wind had shifted a we had swung a quarter of a circle, the li stretching far out on our beam gave me a bit a fright, but I went forward and found I cou easily hold the boat by one hand on the chai I took in the lead and dropped it again, a satisfied myself that we were not moving, a finally turned in so thoroughly reassured that slept until six and was very unwilling to get even then. However, the wind began to make rowdy hullabaloo overhead, and at half-past s I turned out sleepily to find that it was blowir hard from the S.E., dead against us.

I had been told that the channel was impossib for a sailing vessel against the wind and that th local sailors never attempt it, but wait at th entrance till the wind will take them throug this being the reason why yesterday we had m such a number of sail all together. Still we ha

false squeamishness about dropping bac
we should find ourselves engaged on a
bit of work.

One can always find a good enoug
for doing anything that one has made
mind to do.   In this case I had a pei
quite apart from the fact that we did
staying where we were, and that the
been so good that we had eaten all the l
could get no more till we should come to
There was a reason *pro* and a reason
everything, in fact, that the human mine
when it is putting up a pretence of beir.
The wind looked like continuing, but,
I could see through the long-distance
there was not yet much current about
buoys, which, however, were standing v
out of the water, tatters of seaweed cl
them far above the waterline showing tl
normal depth.   I was sure of two things:
that a strong current would be setting a
out of the Sound within a very few hours
second, that I should have to deal wit
abnormally low.   The first outweighed th
and at seven in the morning our anchoi
and hanging at our bows, ready to dro
moment in case of need, and we were c
back to the fairway, the lead going all th
two fathoms of water.   Then we beat up
the two spar-buoys that mark the entran

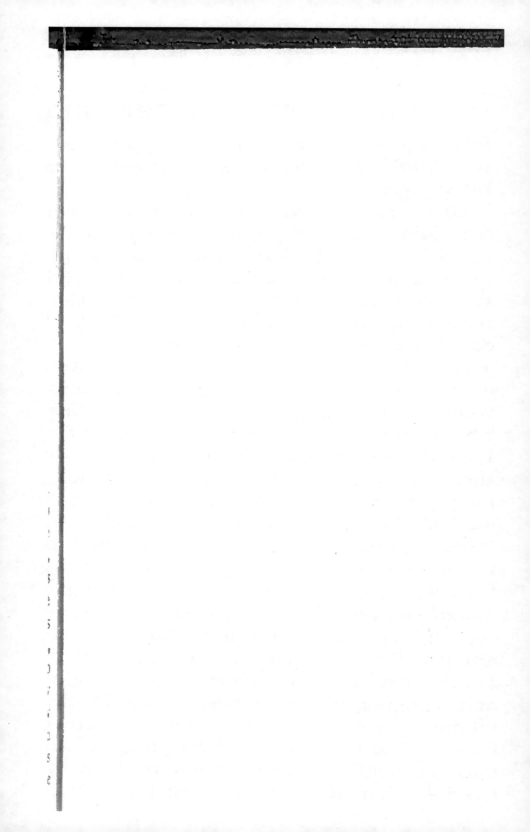

HAPSAL JETTY (SHOWING LEADING BEACONS).

shoulders with expression. But, though *Racun*
is not good at beating as compared with rac
yachts, she is better against the wind than a
of the local cutters and schooners, and, when
set her at it this morning, she seemed to kn
she was expected to do her best, and did
There was a toughish wind too, and that alw:
suits her. With less wind·we should not h:
tried it. At the same time, we left nothing
chance and took no risks of her missing sta
which, in this narrow way between rocks a
sharply shoaling banks, would have meant alm
inevitable disaster. I had sweated over the ch
till I knew it pretty well by heart, and ind
only looked at it twice, and that when we w
already through the actual channel and were (
again in more or less open water, looking for
buoys and beacons that show the way into Hap
Bay. I therefore set the Ancient at the til
and went forward myself with the lead line han
though as a matter of fact there was never ti
to use it and it would have been useless, beca:
there is no gradual shoaling. You are either
the channel with three fathoms of water or (
of the channel with a fathom or less, or on
rock with no more than a couple of feet.
real business forward was to deal with the st:
sail in getting her quickly about and to con t
little ship in without, if I could help it, co
municating to the Ancient any of the doubts w
which I was myself beset.

" Ready about " in a tone as near as
that in which those words are spoken ʋ
are at sea and have the whole Baltic †
mistakes in.   At first the Ancient was jus⸱
bit petulant at the frequency of our ta
we touched once with the centreboar
hanging on an extra second, once only, a
that moment he was perfect and ev
worked in the delirious, exciting manner
rope walking.   He knew then that we rea
on a tightrope, and that this was not an
of my ridiculous preference for imaginir
navigating, that *Racundra* has the dra
a big ship.   We swung round as the woɪ
out of my mouth; I had the staysail al
the mainsail filled, and we were off again,
from side to side of the channel, makir
every time, creeping up in hurried ziɡ
dozen or so between each buoy.   The chaɪ
had read so often in the winter took visi⸱
shape as we moved.   There was Mereholn
those rocks awash; there the two windɪ
Nukke; there, at last, the buoy with a ball
brooms' bases apart on the top.   The brc
not there, but that must be the buoy none

It is hard enough to give an idea of hoʋ
looked.   At first, of course, there was t⸱
sea behind us, and we were pushing our
between the wooded island of Worms ⸱
low, grass-patched and rocky mainlan⸱

sail so near those brown rocks with such a sp
of open water on the other side. How m
simpler to sail boldly up the middle. And th
on the other tack, just a few score yards, of
less, and there were more rocks under the wa
or pale green shallows splashed with dark, and
were thankfully about again and scuttling b
towards the brown lumps that at least w
out of water and less secretive in their villai
And yet, what a stretch of water! and rot
Racundra would go again, the wavelets foe
ing under her bows, and so on, to and fro, a
to fro, each time gaining a little southwa
against the wind, through gusts of which
had to yell to be heard by the Ancient at
tiller.

I had enjoyed following the intricate Mt
Sound channel from Paternoster through by
Erik Stone and Harry island to the open s
but there big ships could go, and we had a mar;
of yards and sometimes far more, in case
left it for a moment. Here there was no mar;
at all. We were ourselves drawing with cent
board down (as we had to have it down for beati
against the wind) more than most of the sm
coasters who alone use this channel. It v
incredibly exciting, the more so that as we p
ceeded, and time went on and the wind still ble
there was visibly growing current against
from the S. through the channel. It beca

it ? [1]   Each spar-buoy left astern was a
triumph, and I would hardly let myself
that we had left the worst of the channe
us until the view before us had already
and we could see far into the broad Soun
hull-down   were   three   goose-winged   s
hurrying from the S. before the wind
them was a friendly ally, the same wi
Racundra, sailing from the N., had
meet and conquer. Now, after just fou
of frenzied beating, we were making long
keeping our eyes on two tall beacons
mainland on the southern side of Hap:
already within the mouth of the inl
watching to bring two other beacons in li
Hapsal town with its church and ruine
Those two beacons, one on shore and one
of a rock almost awash, would lead u
between the shallows towards the little
harbour, on the quay of which again
other beacons which, taken in line, help lit
through the last few hundred yards
passage. We shifted from the line of
pair to the line of the second, found t.
buoys that supplement these land signs, a
sailing E. with the wind free, fairly foam

[1] I am told by hydrographers that it is probably in
say that the wind *causes* the current through these
They say that wind and current are alike *caused* by
or the lack of it, elsewhere. To the simple sailorme

buoy to buoy until at noon we rounded up a
anchored beside two small trading cutters ab
a cable's length from Hapsal pierhead.

*   *   *   *   *

Here we lay for two nights, waiting for a f
wind, and used the intervening day of brig
sunshine for the drying of bedding and mattres
and for a visit to the town, which is some lit
way from the jetty. Indeed, as you approa
Hapsal from the sea, the jetty, with the tall wh
granary behind it, looks like an island, for i
narrow strip of land that connects it with
town is flat and low. The town itself is group
round a low hillock on which is a ruined cas
which has, so we learnt, its ghosts and its Hour
of Hell guarding hidden treasure, all indeed tl
is necessary and fitting for a ruin in a popu
watering-place.

The castle was the residence of the Germ
bishops who, during the thirteenth century, ma
themselves the first foreign rulers of Esthor
The revolting Ests tried in vain to take it in 13
Two hundred years and more after that it v
taken by the Swedes. They did not hold it
long, for the Swedish officer commanding had
money to pay his troops, and so, in those go
old days of private initiative, pawned the cas
to his soldiers on the understanding that, if th
pay did not arrive by the next Midsummer's D
they could sell the castle to whom they cho

and did actually sell the castle for forty t
talers to Ungern, who was acting viceroy
King of Denmark.   Next year the Russia
it for nothing and without meeting any re:
for which reason the Danish leader, Sta
duly executed in Arensburg.   Ten years l:
Russians, after a fight, lost it to the Swe(
in 1628 the Swedish King, improving
commercial methods of the Swedish soldi(
it for 66,830 talers to a Field-Marshal, wl
died in the utmost poverty after his
purchase had been quietly reappropriated
Crown, who perhaps were thinking of s(
again.   But the Swedes held on to the]
too long, for before they tried to sell it
time, Peter the Great in 1710 made it]
and Russian it remained until 1918, whe1
occupied by the Germans, on whose d(
the Ests came at last into their own.

We had this ruin to see and, beside
needed bread, milk, meat and matches, a
set our hearts on a cabbage, which we]
been able to find in Baltic Port.   So, after
in the early morning, we walked in over
slip of land, that would certainly be cov
high water if this were not a tideless s
came to the town—a little town with
streets   of   stone   and   wooden   houses,   t
about   round   the   shallow   inlets   of   wat
from   one   promontory   to   another   in   a

but in all the years of my acquaintance w
them I have never met one who knew how
tell me the way. They will point vaguely in i
wrong direction, or, if they point in the rig
direction, will tell you, as a landmark, to lc
out for a tree with a broken branch among seve
hundreds all with broken branches, instead
mentioning a large, obvious barn which a bli
man could not miss. Here, in Hapsal, we fou
the further difficulty that the cosmopolitan seas
was over and that therefore everybody had ceas
to understand any language but Esthonian.
was there once for a few days earlier in t
summer, when most people seemed to know bc
Russian and German. Now, it was as if eve
linguist in the place had gone into hibernati
till next spring. We did, however, at last co
out in the middle of the town, where we fou
two hotels. We tried both. In one a man v
viciously tuning a piano. In the other there v
a gramophone. In neither did we see a
visitors besides ourselves, and in both we w
told at once that the season was over, as inde
we were told so by everyone with whom we spo
even by the baker from whom we bought t
bread, as much as to say that we had no busin
to be there. I got the impression that the to
was quite consciously recovering itself, drawing
long breath and enjoying its nationality after t
alien but profitable bustle of the summer.

where whole families go to the seaside
tumultuous fortnight or month of holiday
the men plant out their wives and chi:
Hapsal for the summer, to get brown, ta
baths and cure imaginary diseases, wh:
run down from Reval by train for the we
There is a floating restaurant on the inla
and great consumption of vanilla ices,
open-air concerts, regattas in hired boats—
opportunities for all that such visitors de:
  When *Racundra* sailed in there, a
maelstrom of amusement was still. T
crowds of hypochondriac rheumatics tak
baths and impatiently exchanging sympto
disappeared. The little town was itself
and, if I were to stay there, the back en
year is certainly the time that I should
The tiny market under the castle was
busy in the morning, as no doubt it h
since the Middle Ages. We met there
from the country and the islands in the
costume—bright red bodices, black ac
pleated skirts, with red stockings, shor
socks over the red stockings and black sh
strips of black leather criss-cross over th
socks. And though the visitors were g
boats remained, and, for the crew of *R*
these boats compete with the ruins as th
of most interest in Hapsal.
  I should explain that beyond the pier

and a special type of boat, unlike any others
the Esthonian coast, has been evolved for sai
on it. I have a reproduction of an old draw
showing that boats something like these were
existence in the very early nineteenth century
not earlier. They are shaped a little like
shallow wherries of the Norfolk Broads, but
of course, much smaller. They have a f
sized cabin right forward, with a big well
the passengers and a small well right aft
the steersman, who from that position controls
sails. The mainsail is extremely high and they
sloop-rigged. They have neither centrebo
nor lee-boards, but, drawing not more thar
couple of feet of water, they sail in the n
remarkable manner both off and by the wind.

HAPSAL TO HELTERMAA (ISLAN DAGÖ)

SEPTEMBER 11TH. Barometer 29.9. The w
still against us this morning, shifting
W. and S.W., but a whole day lying at
had made us determined to move, if only
through the difficult bit between the R
and Odroraga reefs, or, if we should fai
that, at least to get to anchorage at I
ready to slip through the moment the wind
change. We got our anchor at 7.30 and,
tacking, passed by the pierhead near en
learn that the fishermen thereon, who ha
before the dawn, had caught two little sil
between them. Then we began with
labour to retrace, as far as the black-an
buoy where the channel from Nukke and
joins that from the S., the course which
run so merrily with the wind free tw
before.

The sun was behind the Hapsal beaco
in the glare over the water they wer
invisible, so we just felt our way out,

together with the rich dark smell of frying bac
At nine we reached the first of the main buoys ;
at ten minutes past ten we were at the th
round which the channel turns to the S. H
we brought *Racundra* to the wind and h
her to while we hauled the dinghy on board.
then tacked on southwards. It was a wearisc
business, but we were all keen to go on, for w
the wind backing to the S.W. we had a g
hope of being able to point straight through
narrow alleyway of buoys between the reefs.
went as close as we dared to the Odroraga ;
saw its wicked line just below the surface of
water, and at one point a little strip of it, p
red above the wavelets, with seabirds hudd
together upon it. We stood away then
Estholm, where are the beginnings and the ru
of a fine harbour, warehouses and quays al
broken by the war, wrecks of half-sunk ponto
lifting desperately into the air and a forlorn cra
A little cutter was at anchor close by the pi
We had watched her through the glasses, pick
her way in with lowered foresail and dropped pe
Away to the E., with the wind behind her, a
schooner was coming easily through the pass
by the Rukeraga beacon. We went about a
sailed close-hauled to meet her.

The beacon is fixed on the northern end o
low strip of rock, just above the level of the wat
The *Baltic Pilot*, by the way, like the Germ

distance, and easily recognisable from
miles away because of the big conical ston€
lie near it. Just N. of it and running·
W. is a narrow lane of four pairs of spa·
The channel between them is not a stone
across, and, as there are rocks and stone :
just outside the line of the buoys on eitl
beating through it is impossible.

We met the schooner, envying her sp
favourable wind, and reaching the first
buoys, found we could just point thro
channel. We passed the first three pairs c
with no difficulty, and were just rejoicing ir
got through a ticklish bit of sailing when I
that, though we were heading by compass a
the wind had fallen a little, and the last
buoys were slipping slowly southwards. I
Racundra's head a fraction up. It m
difference. We were already caught in the
which, sweeping up along the far side of t]
touched us here, whereas it had been imper
during the first three-quarters of the :
There was nothing to be done. There was
time nor room to beat. We were alreac
upon the last pair of buoys, and we were
wrong side of the northern one. I
forward and the Ancient stood by with th€
as a last resource, while we stood on, ou
in our mouths. The buoy was abeam of
visibly slipping away. It was on our ·

were out in the Moon Sound proper, where]
steamers find their way and where beacons :
lit at night. Now we cared for nothing. I
Racundra fall a point off the wind and {
brisked up like a horse after a feed of oats. 1
wind backed a little more and she pointed W.
S. and even W.S.W. That, however, was {
best that she could do, and we were not yet
enough from the reefs to put her about on 1
other tack. So we held on, watching the south(
shore of Worms and recognising far before
the low coast of Dagö island and Pihalep chu1
spire, that is a good guide from afar to the pleas{
little harbour of Heltermaa.

Then the wind strengthened and fell aw.
strengthened and fell away from the S.W.,
short unpleasing sea of the Moon Sound got 1
and the admirable *Racundra* began to sh
us that we had been wrong in boasting that {
did not roll. She rolled abominably. The m
boom swung from side to side with mighty ban
until I lashed it to the lee backstay tackle. 1
mizen boom swung on unheeded. Things w
very unpleasant, and, as we looked back to
tall Rukeraga beacon, seeming now as if it floa
in the water, it was clear enough that we w
making very little southing. If that was so
this part of the Sound, if the current was so str(
here, it would be very much worse in the narr(
to the S., and, anxious as we were to get alo

exiguous Dagö trade, passed us bound (
for Heltermaa. I had been in Helterma
and knew it for a picturesque place, or
smallest good harbours in the world. T
that church on the horizon, a fine mark
by; and, after all, we reasoned, if the wir
change we should be able to consider
to Heltermaa merely as a longer tack. '
lose nothing by going there. So we mad
minds to hold on until either the win
change or we should come to Heltern
wind did not change, so we came to Heltei
before sunset. At 6.15 we warped i
Endla's stern, nearly carrying away
staff as we did so, owing to the energy wi
we were helped by the men of Helterr
found ourselves in very snug quarters
night.

There was room in Heltermaa harbou:
tiny *Hiumaa*, one open fishing-boat, a
Racundra, the *Endla* and a scho
small size. But *Endla* was tied up
the harbour proper, across the end of the
and the schooner was at anchor. The
boat, *Racundra* and *Hiumaa* filled a
able quay berths. A young man in
who was, I think, coastguard, soldier and
master, came on board and enthus
pencilled the date of *Racundra's* arriva
papers. Then, as it looked like rain, we

A hundred yards or so from the harbour is
so-called inn, that was once a Russian postin
station where you could hire horses, at so man
kopecks per mile per horse, to take you acros
the island. It is still called an inn, and peopl
do sleep on sacks of straw there, if they are o
their way to Hapsal and the Sound is too roug
for the little steamer. Its landlord, who has c
had some official connection with the harbou
talks only Esthonian, nor does his wife talk an
other language. My dealings with them wer
not easy. I tried English. I tried Russiar
These failing, I took a long breath and aske
them for milk in Esthonian.

"Piima," I said, and waved my milk-can.

"Ei ole piima," they replied in chorus.

All right. If they had no milk I would try fc
eggs.

"Muna," I said, and the good woman scuttle
off as if she were a hen herself and came bac
with a lot of very little eggs.

"Kui palio maksap?" said I.

"Kumme munat" (ten eggs), said the womar
counting on her fingers. "Nelli kument mark."

"Forty marks." I had only a note for
hundred, and they had no change or very littl
so they gave me ten marks back and a numbe
of new white loaves.

That was all they could do, but that was nc
enough. They pointed up the road towards th
forest, and I went to the next house which turne

an idle hour. I tried English, and sh
the colour of a ripe apple.

" I know English," she said, and pron
her embarrassment, forgot all she knew.

I dare say she reads Shakespeare. I
highly likely that she teaches Engli
understood perfectly when I explained
wanted milk; but when she tried to a
was as if someone held her tongue by
and muffled her brain. By now, I am
has thought out the speech she should ha
At the time she was struck dumb, and
to the doorstep, could only point up
into the forest, turn redder and redder
her pink cotton dress looked almost wl
stammer, " House, house, house, house .
then, with a flash of memory, " YELLOW
So I thanked her and she fled away back
schoolroom, while I went on towards t
looking for a yellow house.

I found the yellow house; but the woma
who talked Esthonian to me, exhausted
explaining that they had only one cow
ten in family. She directed me to anoth
where she said they were few in family
two cows. I found that house; but th
in it said that I could have milk only
cows should come home, and that they
expected home before eight o'clock.
she directed me to another house.

that she had no milk, would not let me go, l
held me firmly by my jersey, and called for l
husband to come out and look. To me she sa
" We have no milk," but to him, " Here is
Englishman," and held me firmly till he came
long, thin, smiling fellow who somehow reminc
me of John Masefield. I accordingly felt frien
towards him, and perhaps I reminded him
someone, for he seemed to feel friendship for r
and took me by the arm and led me to a sta
hedge, where he pulled out a stake to let
through, and said, " Over there is a house w
a little white barn, and there lives a Russian m:
and he has good cows and will certainly give y
milk."

So I wandered on into the forest and came
a house with a little pigsty beside it with a gl
window, the only pigsty with a glass wind
that I can remember to have seen. And beyo
that, sure enough, was a house, a log cabin, w
a tiny barn, and the barn was whitewashed. A
here I spoke to the woman of that house
Russian ; but she did not understand me, and cal
to her husband, who came from the potato-b
wearing his shirt outside his trousers in the Russi
fashion.

With him, of course, I had a good talk and gre
difficulty in coming to business. He told me
had come here as a soldier in the Russian serv
thirty years ago, and had married a wife a

out of it, and indeed in Poltava is the bla
and here is nothing but stone; but now I
years old and a little more, and I am
well, and I do not suppose I shall see
again." Then he told me he had sold all
for the *Endla*; but I let that pass, and
me of how he had been a policeman in I
" a summer policeman," he explained,
winter, it seems, there are no visito
policemen are not necessary—and how
wearing a Cossack *bourka*, or long clo
talking very good Russian, had told him
had played cards with the Emperor. '
clear enough that he was a great man."
put in another word about the milk, and
something to his wife about milk for the
and she laughed, and I guessed that the
on the *Endla* were going to get less
milk than they had hoped, for she took r
can and went off, while he told me th
been great rains, so that the water stood
the potato rows and the potatoes had rot
went on to ask if all was well with I
Then he noticed the eggs that I had bo
the inn. " Those are very little eggs,"
and asked me what I had had to pay fo
I asked him if he had any, as we need
for our ship, and he sent a little girl who
ten beauties, twice the size of those alrea
basket. Then the woman came back v

paid for the eggs and the milk, he asked me
there was nothing else I wanted that he cou
give me, and I could think of nothing; but
gave me the best of his turnips and a lot of fre
beans, and with that he walked with me to ;
opening in the trees, whence we could see tl
harbour and *Racundra's* two masts. "If tho
masts are there in the morning," said he, " n
wife shall bring you some more milk."

And so we parted, thanking each other, like o
friends, and I hurried back by a quick way I
showed me across country and came to the shi
and found that those hungry ones had finishe
supper and that my supper was cold, but I a
it with great pleasure, full of the warmth of th
abundance of human intercourse.

" TOLEDO " OF LEITH

THE last time I was at Heltermaa wa
before we sailed in there in *Racundra,*
came there on foot, after walking from
side of the island, where I had landed fro1
timber-carrying schooner in which I h:
from the mainland. I came to Helterm:
road from Kerdla, and was hurrying back
the *Kittiwake* at Baltic Port. It so
that I came there on a day when there
means of getting across the Sound to
and I was disconsolately trying to arra
the innkeeper to let me sleep the night on
when two sailors came in buying provi
tried them in my own language. One
knew a few words, and told me that th
of his ship spoke English, and that I h
come with them. I asked him where his
and he pointed far out to sea, where, sur
a large steamship was lying.

I helped the men to carry a sack of
a tin of kerosene, milk, butter, bread an(
little pig down to the tiny harbour. Th
small open boat with a jib and sprit

took the tiller, the other dealt with the sails, a I nursed the little pig. Within half an hour of trudging into Heltermaa I was at sea, slipp rapidly over the four or five miles that separ Heltermaa from the Erik Stone.

As we came nearer, I was surprised at the v the ship was lying, broadside on to the wind a perfectly steady, across breaking waves. She v aground. Then, as we came nearer yet, I s that her shrouds were dangling round the ma and that she had been stripped bare. She v not, as I had supposed, a passing ship send ashore for provisions. She was a wreck. I asl how long she had been there. "Two ye or more. We are waiting for high water," s the man.

There was a rising wind, and we approach the wreck at great speed, shot round under l stern, luffed, lowered the sails and caught h of a rope-ladder. As we came round under l stern I looked up for the name and read, "TOLED LEITH." Here in this most unexpected of plac was a British ship. I ran up the ladder a climbed over the bulwarks and down on the rus shell of what once upon a time had steamed all the pride of new paint and shining brasswo out of the Firth of Forth.

A small boy was hanging some fishing-nets dry. He pointed aft when I asked for the capta and, bending to avoid the nets and fishing-lir

me in English, invited me into his cabin,
I must stay the night with him, and pror
put me over to the mainland in the morn

I have seen many cabins, but none q
that hutch in which the captain of the *Tc*
his comfortable being.　It was built of b
wood set up on end between the iron de
was six feet six inches high, long and broa
size, Captain Konga explained, he had f
experiment to be the most convenient.
on his bunk, he could put wood on the
the corner, light his reading-lamp, take
from the opposite shelf, eggs or bacon :
store-cupboard, reach down his saucepan c
pan from the hooks on the wall, or get t
swain's whistle, with piercing blasts of \
summoned the members of his crew.　F₁
place in it he could reach every other pl
that, he said, was the most labour-saving
house.

He told me the story of the ship.　She]
captured by the Germans in the summer
She had been aground on the shallows
Heltermaa, but one wild night, while the
had all been drinking ashore, a strong
wind had so raised the waters in the C
the *Toledo* floated off, and when the
came to look for her in the morning,
floated far out to sea, and by miraculou

taken her over and Captain Konga had come
live on board. Once only, in the previous winf
she had floated for a few minutes, but the iccbe
round her were so thick that with the instrume
at his command he could not shift her, and ·
sinking water had left her again in her pla
To-day the water was rising again. "Anot
four inches and we shall have her moving," s
Captain Konga, and showed me the cables
had laid out astern, the little boiler and donk
engine he had brought from Reval, and his ot
arrangements for pulling her into deep water ·
moment she should float. Actually, as we st
there, we could feel that she was on the point
floating. He had a marked pole over the si
and from time to time looked at it, to see if ·
water was still rising.

"Yet she isn't worth much, nowadays,"
said. "The Germans stripped her of some thin
and when they went the local pirates did ·
rest. They took everything, even pulling ·
engines to pieces to get the nuts. Nuts m⟨
good sinkers for fishing-nets. The portholes h⟨
all gone. All the new schooners built on Wor
have fine brass portholes made in Edinburgh.'

And here for two years Captain Konga had b⟨
living and enjoying himself most mightily.
shot seals which came and played by the ro
He painted the rock red. He shot duck. He fish
All passing boats took supplies of fresh fish fr⟨

ringing the changes on these five. He was d
to talk English, and told me he had a friend
land, a very pretty young woman, living ne
He had taught her Russian and she had
him English.   " A very pretty young w
said he.   I asked him when he had last s
and he told me, twenty-five years ago.   ]
liked to suggest that the young womar
now be older, for he seemed so certain 1
her at least time had stood still.   " And so
he added, " and so active.   Runs like a h:
dances . . . you should see her dance ! "

Time, for Captain Konga, did not exist
that he never had quite enough of it fc
wished to do.   When I offered to send hir
papers, thinking foolishly that he migh
them, living alone out there on the wre
Heltermaa as his metropolis, and tha
approachable in fine weather in his little
thanked me, but said he would never ha
to read them, his life was so busy, wh
birds, seals, fish, and the making of ca
and nets and fishing-lines, drying, salt:
skinning.   He was enjoying himself enoi
and, as we talked, I perceived that he
had enjoyed himself enormously, looking
before nor after, but whole-heartedly eng
whatsoever he was doing.   And he had done
things, hunting bears in the Arctic, hunted
by the women of the Samoyede madd

thirty years ago as if they had happened tl
same afternoon.

Next day it blew so hard that it was alm
impossible to stand on deck, except in the shel
of the bulwarks, so I spent another night w
Captain Konga, netting, and hearing tales of
Esthonian coast, of Ungern Sternberg and
wreckers, of the people of the Tutters islan
who will not let the Salvage Company appro;
a wreck before the men of Tutters have finisl
with it. "The sea was black with their lit
boats, and as I came near with a tug, they shou
at me to keep off, and waved every man a ;
to show that they were armed." "But that ;
a long time ago," said I. "It was last year, or
year before. These people do not change so f;
I've had to show that we have guns to keep th
off the *Toledo*. The Dagö folk are quiet enou
but the men of Worms . . . and the men
Worms are sucking babes beside the pirates
Tutters."

On the second morning the sea was going do
and the wind was less, and the captain and
of his men lowered away the little skiff that
had for fishing. There was just room for the tl
of us in her. We sailed due E. to the island
Worms, thinking that I should there catch
postman's cutter for Hapsal. We came u
patches of rocks, awash and out of the wa
Then the man lowered the sprit. reducing

Then out in deep water again, and the litt
which was Captain Konga's special prid€
slipped across the waves. We landed on the
corner of Worms by Sviby, but the posᵢ
had gone, and the captain looked at his
It was just possible that we might catch t]
at Hapsal. We were off again, but as
came in sight saw the train steaming in the
It is nearly two miles from the pier to the
The thing could not be done. " How many
have we ? " asked the captain. I told him.
nothing, but turned aside from the fairway
to the pier and steered straight across th
shoals at the station. We touched once,
and sat every moment expecting to gro┌
good. But luck was with us, as it must al┐
with such as Captain Konga, and with two ₁
to spare he ran the boat ashore and I jum
the train.

That autumn the water gave him his
and he took it, pulled *Toledo* off, and with t
of a tug from Reval took her to Helsing
felt sorry for him when I heard it. As a
ship, in these days, I do not suppose the
was worth much, nor would his share of ᵢ
large. But as a fishing and shooting bo>
man like him, who knew how to use every ɪ
of his time in such pursuits, she was wiᵗ
better in the world.

A HOUSE ON MOON.

FROM THE ISLAND OF DAGÖ TO TI ISLAND OF MOON

At Heltermaa we were to stay for longer than wished. We lay there from the 12th to the 1' of September, watching the barometer and ? sky and getting sharp pains in the backs of ? necks from looking up the mast at the wimp which for all that time showed us a wind in ? teeth, while, as we could see from the bow spar-buoys outside, there was a current to ma it. To beat S. against wind and stream was ho less. So we lay there and talked of how when ? own wind came we would fly southward throu the Moon Sound and then run from end to end the Riga Gulf in a single twenty-four hours. Wl our wind came we actually did that run in ma hours less, and most of it under almost bare po but our wind was a long time in coming. Meanwl there was plenty of wind of the wrong sort, wh blew our flag to pieces and unravelled it u there was hardly any of it left. The Ancient m: a new long wimpel from a strip of red bunti and when I joked with him for hoisting a Bolshe flag replied: "It'll give the wind a fright ?

half a gale from the S.E., and a heav
came through the wooden piles of the pie
schooner from Worms had warped into tl
to load apples and we had shifted to mak
and then tied up to the schooner, hoping fo
protection. But that night, at two o'clock
morning, a loud crack brought me on deck, l
and in pyjamas, to meet the Ancient, w
tumbled up out of the forehatch at th
moment, and the two of us, just in time,
on a rope with all the strength we ha
Racundra, while we fixed a new warp to
the stout one that had parted. It had
through in spite of heavy parcelling, anc
after we not only served and parcelled i
it crossed the schooner's railing, but sp
as if it were a broken limb, binding chips
wood round it, so that it lay snug in a
shell. Even that had worn thin before
but the rope was kept in perfect conditi(
the dodge is one to recommend to any oth
cruisers in such circumstances.

Not all the inhabitants of Dagö were as
to us as those with whom I had talked (
first evening. Some are stern patriots, an
their feelings by refusing to talk the lai
which, until in 1919 they became indep
had been imposed on them by force. All t
us knew a few words of Esthonian and mac

He had said " Good-day " to us in Esthonian on(
and we had replied in Esthonian, for politene.
sake, and perhaps from pride in this small scr
of our uncertain vocabulary. But next day, wh
he came again, the Ancient, talking Russia
tried to learn from him where he could buy me:
and the Esthonian flushed red and angry, a:
asked him what he was talking Russian for, wh
he had shown the day before that he could ta
Esthonian as well as himself. The poor Ancie
tried to make him believe that he knew how
say " Good-morning," but did not know how to s
anything else, but the Esthonian would not
appeased, turned his back on him and took
a fine Napoleon attitude on the pierhead, " as i
said the Ancient, " he would like to be the sto
figure of a patriot." Unfortunately, however,
was not content with being a stone figure, I
tried to persuade others of his fellow-countrym
to have no dealings with us except in Esthoni:
After that there were two factions among 1
people who came down to the quay—the patri(
who would have nothing to do with us and 1
cosmopolitans who sold us what they had a
made us presents of ripe apples and worms
our fishing, and, when in the middle of the nig
the little steamer came from Reval, woke us
with shouts from the quay, lest we should m
our share of the general happy excitement. 1
two factions came often to hot words, and amc

what a small nation must feel while its fate
discussed by greater Powers.

During the days when we were not
and, since the wind from the south was
the bait in the fishes' mouth, catching p
good fish supper, we walked on the islar
found a great number of fossils on the
stone sponges and petrified shells of
shapes. We also found lucky stones, with
holes in them, like (but how different fro:
lucky stone on *Racundra's* cabin wall, th
from Coniston and the friendliest house in I
It was warm in the sunshine and I saw
woodpecker, but he is with us all the year, a
other signs it was only too clear that wir
falling swiftly upon us. The starlings were
flocks. The leaves on the trees were turn
the nights were growing long. The very
that were being brought down to the (
little springless carts and carefully packe
in the hold of the schooner beside us were a
that the days were coming when, in these
at any rate, little ships cannot keep the se
Ancient began talking with persistent gloor
" the Equinotion time," when the Gulf (
would be at its very worst. The autumn
of September 23rd was indeed close at han
we were held here as if by some malice of
to wait for its notorious inhospitality.

However, when we had begun to thin

tember 16th there was a breath of wind fro
the W. We hardly dared to trust it, but, wi
faint hope, set alarm clocks to wake us ear
At half-past six next morning the wind freshen
from the W. again, and ten minutes later
were swinging from the end of the pier on a sing
warp while we hoisted sail. Five minutes aft
that, with main and mizen set, we cast off, rejoici
like prisoners released, and running up our sta
sail when we were already under way. By half-pa
seven we were well out into the Sound, and bo
up on the starboard tack to pass about a m
E. of the island of Heinlaid. Thence we steer
S. by E. and ¾ E., looking for the bell-buoy in t
middle of the Sound.

The wind was one to stir the blood and we wo
all in the best of spirits, taking it in turns to
below and eat great quantities of porridge, wh
we sighted a biggish steamer coming up from t
S., with buff funnel and black top to it, a
the peculiar bows that belong to our friend t
Baltabor. As she came nearer, however, the Ancie
whose eyes are usually better than mine, decic
that she was not the *Baltabor* but a Germ;
" Yet her bows are awfully like," I said, " thou
she has hardly had time to go to England a
back since she steamed out of Reval harbour w
the Pelorus she had promised to lend us still
board." These words I said as I turned to
below, but I was not half-way down the compan

sent a man to the jack staff. Up goes o
flutters at the mizen top, dips half-way
up again, while our big friend's ensign,
broad as our mainsail, does the same. I
very pleasantest of greetings between
and little British ships meeting each oth
cold, sunny September morning on a sea
unlike the seas of England. Moreover,
doing 5.6 knots at the time, and that was
satisfaction, as the last occasion on which
had seen us under sail was when we we
tacking through the Mühlgraben by Riga
were afraid she might have been given
notion of our speed.

We sighted our bell-buoy close on the
just where it should have been, and this,
with *Baltabor* and the sun and the bl
and the keen air and the wind that suited
from truck to keel, all combined to
delighted with ourselves and Fate. But w
Fate on the back too soon. " We shall b
to-morrow," we cried, as we saluted the
triumphantly, and steered southwards to l
beacons of the island of Moon in a line.
as we did so, we found we were standin
close-hauled. The wind was backing tc
again. We were now retracing the course
followed when running up from Patern
the outward voyage, and at 10.45 pa
Moon light-buoy. finished with the Moon

THE GATES OF MOON.

Kuivast anchorage, to bring up there and s
what was going to happen next. The aged cutt
that plies as ferry-boat between Kuivast and t
mainland passed on the port tack close acrc
our bows and then went about. We raced the
for the anchorage and beat them, anchoring
12.30 close off the pier at Kuivast in two fathon
stiff clay bottom, and getting our sails down
time to watch the cutter bring up to the pi
Here were a number of cattle awaiting it, and v
saw for the first time the fiery orange petticoa
and black bodices which are the national costun
of the women of Moon. We watched the wom(
go on board with their cattle, and then, as it w
clear that we were in for another southerly stori
put the covers on the sails. We had made goc
something over twenty-five miles.

There is no harbour at Kuivast, nothing but
short pier, crooked at the outer end, but enclosir
so small a space that even the little steame
never attempt to enter it. The ferry-cutter tic
up inside to load cattle, but had only just roor
the rest of the space being occupied by two sma
waterlogged barges. The anchorage immediate
off the pier is very good, as far as holding capacit
goes, but very bad as regards protection. W
learnt later that we had dropped our anchor in tl
best possible place, as farther south the rock
very near the surface. Indeed, a schooner th:
anchored there dragged her hook and had to sper

N.W. This is not so. With both south
northerly winds, owing perhaps to some tri
variable current, the swell rushes across
and breaks over the Kuivast pier. Both
and German charts mark this place as
anchorage. For smaller vessels, however,
now a very much better stopping place
other side of the Sound. Of that, how
knew nothing when we arrived.

The orange-petticoated women drove the
into the cutter, and for some time a few
men of Moon watched us from the pierh
presently, as it began to blow harder, 1
women alike went off to the shelter of the
down houses. It was not till late in the a:
when the wind slackened, that the cutter
fit to sail, when it made straight across th
to some landing place on the other side
not wishing to lose the chance of sayin
had at least talked with some of the p
Moon, I made up my mind to go ashoi
Ancient helped me to sling the dinghy o
with the fore-halyard, and I tumbled in
milk-can and pulled for the landing place.

Under the wall of a half-ruined cotta
to the shore was a bench, and on it were
the men of Moon, or rather, three men
and a policeman in a neat grey uniform,
me that he, too, was a foreigner in this pla
he had not been born on Moon, but on t

and I heard him announce his discovery to t
others. Then I tried Russian, and found he cou
talk Russian just about as badly as I talk it myse
The others knew only two or three words of t
language, but, unlike the patriots of Helterma
they were willing enough to use the words th
knew, and, indeed, put them eagerly, by way
punctuation marks, into the conversation betwe
the policeman and myself.

The policeman was a delightful fellow: ask
where we were going, praised the speed of o
little ship as compared with that of the ferry-cutt
told me not to use the water from the well 1
the pier, because it and everything cooked with
would taste of seaweed, but to take water fro
the other well by the inn. " At least," he sai
lest he should raise false hopes, " it used to 1
an inn." When I asked for milk, he volunteer
at once to take me to this ci-devant tavern, an
in case the man there or his wife did not unde
stand, to translate for me. With that we saunter
up the muddy lane together and passed witho
ceremony through the stone Gates of Moon.

From *Racundra's* deck I had seen these tw
strange stone columns on either side of the roa
leading inland from the pier, and had asked th
Ancient what he made of them.

" Those," said he, " mighta be the Gates (
Moon, of which I have often heard tell. The baror
that lived here did all for themselves as them

This sounded a little too much like Huc
account of kings, so I had gone ashore
open mind.

I asked the policeman what the pillars
"There are a lot of fairy tales abou
said he, "but I think myself that they
up in honour of the Emperor Nicolas I.
visited the island of Moon."

That explanation at least was one of
tales.　The Ancient had been nearer th
Beside the pillars I now noticed a stor
Cross and pillars alike seemed to be of a
same age, something near 1600, I shoul
but fixed on one of the pillars was
placard of later date, perhaps eighte
early nineteenth century.　This placard
German and Russian and set out a tariff
so much for a carriage, so much for a
much for a peasant's cart, so much for
so much for a peasant's cow, so muc
man, and, finally, so much for a dog
must have been some lively incidents
attempted collection of tolls from sportive,
dogs, who might run in and out ten tim
many minutes while the toll-keeper was
with larger folk.　The actual sums demar
been obliterated.　On the other pillar, opp
tariff, was a coat of arms, I believe that o
German castle town of Arensburg, a fat anc

Russia on finding that the Russian Empire
them a freer hand in exploiting the Esthoni
than was given them by the more liberal-min
Swedes.

The Gates were the last symbol of the Germ
civilisation. The inn was the last symbol of
Russian. It was a typical Russian posting stati
a low, one-storied building, with pillars along
front of it, where, as throughout Russia o
seven crowded years ago, it was possible to
bad food and good horses and a night's lodgi
the quality of which depended on the thickness
your skin. The Russian stoves were still the
So were the great beds, where from a dozen
twenty people could sleep together on straw or h
The little counter, where the Imperial vodka w
once sold, remained. But there were no hors
no vodka, no sleepers—nothing, in fact, of forn
glory. The innkeeper, who seemed to be a
harbourmaster, told me that he had once h
some beer, but that there was none left. Or
upon a time, he said, he had had some local kv
Now he had nothing except . . . he pointed to
few packets of cigarettes. He had no tobacc
The policeman and I drank a couple of glasses
clear cold water, handed by the innkeeper ov
the counter where so many gallons of vodka h
passed in days gone by. He then showed me t
well, the only one, as both innkeeper and policem
enthusiastically agreed, where the water is fit f

went off and milked a cow, and gave me
full of admirable milk, two quarts of it, 1
Esthonian marks, the value of which in
money would be about fourpence.   Witl
returned to the ship.

KUIVAST TO WERDER

I HAD a hard job not to spill the milk as
pulled back to *Racundra*. The wind was pipi
up again from the S.W. and the swell of which
have already spoken was beginning to come
Racundra was jerking about in so lively a mann
that I decided to put out our larger anchor (six
seven pounds) on the stout coir cable. The Ancie
and I, hauling together, had as much as we cou
do in pulling the ship up towards the first anch
We did this with the tiller lashed over, giving h
something of a sheer, so that we should not
dropping the second anchor on the chain.
then let go and veered out fifteen fathoms or mo
of cable and chain. We lay in two fathoms, amp
for we draw only a little over half a fathom wi
our centreboard up. We then had supper a
turned in.

But we got little rest that night. The wi
increased to a gale, and, sheltered though
were, the current kept *Racundra* across both wi
and swell, with the result that she rolled me o
of my bunk on the top of the big iron pump th
was stowed on the floor, sent things adrift th

be done was to sit on the bunks, wedg
knees firmly against the centreboard-ca
count how many rolls *Racundra* could acc
in a minute. Again and again the Ancien
crawled over the deck to see if we were d
We took the covers off again, and had ev
ready to make sail in a moment, but did r
to do so unless obliged, as we did not the
where to seek shelter without going right
Heltermaa. *Racundra* rolled until she too
on her decks over the railings, in spite of her
freeboard. But the anchors held and :
found us still desperately rolling, in a sw
was splashing over the pier and made us g
we had, according to our custom, taken the
inboard for the night. It was too rough to
the little boat again. The motion was su
we could not cook, nor even make tea.
lived on cold bacon, tinned herrings ar
and relieved our feelings by punchi
barometer.

In the afternoon there was less win
barometer had fallen to 29.2, but now
just the faintest inclination to rise, and
o'clock, as there were patches of sunshine
ashore and took photographs, though it
blowing in gusts that made it very hard
the camera steady. An hour later, how
wind dropped suddenly, and the Ancien

THE NEW HARBOUR AT WERDER.

side of the Sound. She had not reappeared, so
was sure that she had on the other side a bett
shelter than was to be found here. I learnt th
during the war a new harbour had been built
Werder, of which all my charts were ignora
I got rough sailing directions. " Steer straig
across for the southernmost of three white ruin
houses, and when you come near you will see t
harbour and can go into it. There are twelve fe
of water and tugs have wintered there."

This sounded promising, so when in the morni
after a rather better night, we found a bright da
but with wind and strong current still against
from the S., I had the sails up soon af
breakfast and we went across the Sound in plet
of time to come back if we should be disappoin
in what we should find there. The cutter, held
yesterday by the bad weather, had returned
Kuivast, taken on board more red cattle a
orange petticoats, and set sail on her way ba
just after we started. There was enough wi
however, to make *Racundra* a fast boat, and
had the wind on our beam, so we kept them w
astern until we had gone far enough to see a dece
looking harbour with a schooner's masts above
but nothing to show on which side was the ent
When I can use local knowledge, I always pre
it to my own ignorance, so, much to the cutte
astonishment, I brought *Racundra* to the wi
have her to and waited for them to catch

had perceived some special danger ahead
stared with all their eyes. At last, howev
went on, and giving them a fair start, w(
staysail draw and proceeded after them.
we did so, the wind, which had been m
strengthened with a sudden squall, so tha
and *Racundra* alike fairly foamed across
maining distance. We saw that the cutter
to northwards of the harbour mole, so we
same, and a minute or two later had
into as fine a little harbour for small ship:
I hope to see. We anchored and then, dec
stay, ran a warp out to the pier and bertl
selves under the shelter of a huge stack
logs, which, since they were much weatl
concluded had been there some time ar
not likely to fly about our heads.

We had found this harbour of Werder, or
as the Esthonians call it, just in time. Th
the wind came from the N.W. with r:
such violence that the waves breaking on t
flung great bits of themselves not only c
mole but clean over the woodpile, fifte
across and as many high, and down witl
splashes on *Racundra's* cabin roof on th
side. A big open cutter, rather like the fer:
lying beside us was half filled during th
by the water tossed across the mole. At
the morning the wind was blowing from

of fifty little fish—*killos*, boneless little creatur
like sardines, extremely good to eat. I also h:
a pleasant talk with an elderly Robinson Crus(
master and owner of a little open boat, small
even than *Racundra*, who was doing his best
get his things dry after the tempestuous nigh
He had spent the summer carrying stones
Reval, and now was sailing home for the winter
in his own little boat to a bay some half a doz
miles south of Werder. His boat was filled wi
all manner of treasure acquired during the summ
—bits of old iron, empty bottles, a lump or two
good oak, salt, tobacco and other valuables. T
salt and such things he stowed in a cuddy forwai
He slept under his sails and cooked on a little op
stove in the stern. He was plucking a duck :
his dinner when I got into talk with him.]
had shot it the day before, while sheltering behi
a little rocky island farther north. He showed i
his gun, a fowling-piece that might have been t
envy of Man Friday. He knew a little Engli:
having sailed three years on English ships.]
also knew Lettish, a rare accomplishment amo
Esthonians, in whose folklore devils talk Letti
to each other, which is also the language spok
in hell. He had travelled enough to lose su
national prejudices, and sat there, plucking a
cooking his duck, talking with obvious pride wi
the Ancient and me, with each in his own langua;
In the calm of the evening he put to sea, and t

rain squalls, we feared for him, but there
need. He knew the coast, as he had told
the palm of his hand; and the lighthous
who visited us in the morning, told us
had seen the little boat both at dusk ar
and that our friend had spent the nigh
in smooth water behind some rocks, wi
waves on every hand.

The next day the wind was from t
and for the next five days swung to
blowing nearly all the time with tremendc
For all that time the ferry-cutter was u
cross from Werder to Kuivast.   Peasa
Werder and the mainland and men of M
their orange-skirted dames came to the
and day after day hung desolately ak
cutter in wind and rain, at night getti
shelter they could in the forest. " Thi
Equinotion time," said the Ancient ph
cally, " and this is what musta be."   He,]
could afford to be philosophic, for he had 1
berth tight and comparatively dry, and
much better off than the unfortunate :
waiting in the woods for the ferry to ta
home.

It was a wild time. Late one evening we
a ·big schooner, close-hauled, trying to n
entrance of the Sound from the south. (]
during a north-wester.) As she came she
nearer the wind and made less and less h

filled again, while the schooner lost ground. Final
with jibs wildly flogging, she let go her anch
Down came the sails one after another, and
watched her heaving half her length out of t
water, dipping her nose under and rearing aga
The anchor held for ten minutes. Then, not slow
as with dragging anchor, but in a sudden ru:
with parted cable, she was swept away southwai
behind the point, broadside on, a helpless thii
just as dark fell. What became of her I do r
know. The lighthouse-keeper told us that she (
not go on the rocks, but was swept clear of th(
to the south. He saw no attempt made to hc
sail. "They were tired out," he said, "tii
beyond work, and seeing they were drifting cle
perhaps made up their minds to let her drift ·
forty miles south, when they would maybe
rested and have a chance of getting into shel
in the Pernau bight."

During that same blow, another schooner un(
jib and reefed foresail, coming from the nor
swept at terrific speed into our harbour, let
her anchor without standing upon the order of
going, far too near the shore, and, while it dragg(
rowed desperately in their small boat and ma
fast a warp to the pier with perhaps ten secor
to spare in saving her. The men from the otl
schooner that had been there when we arriv
jumped to lend a hand, and she was presen
berthed alongside the quay. The men of t

four or five sacks stuffed into each rick
springless cart.   They also brought the
sheep, which was killed and skinned on
and its flesh then cut up, weighed, paid
put into a barrel with salt, provision
voyage.   They were taking the corn to P
The other schooner here was loading fire
Reval.

There was nothing to be done with the
for though now and again the wind veere
wards it always backed swiftly to th
while the sea remained in frothy tumult.
as if the Equinox had amused himself b
N.W. and S.W. to fight each other, a
one and now the other got the maste
struggle the tension of which hardly slack
a moment.   I made a curve of our b
readings on squared paper during that w
it might have been taken for a graphic r
the progress of a grasshopper.   When we
Werder the barometer was at 29.28.   Af
it bobbed up and down between 29 an
It had been 29.9 when we left Hapsal to
this bout of bad weather.   Often it wa
impossible to stand on the quay, and
thankful for our woodpile, behind whi
comparative peace.   There was no village
than six miles away, and we ran out of egg
potatoes, bread and, worst of all, tobacc
few houses by the old pier that was use

picture of it still reproduced on the English cha
but is a plain wooden framework replacing
old tower, which was blown up during the v
The lighthouse-keeper lives with his wife and th
children in a wooden shanty close by, on a desol
spit of bare ground running out from the wo
into the sea. He used to come and sit in the ca
of *Racundra* and I used to visit him in his shar
The only blemish on his conversation was th
like his brother of Runö, similarly isolated fr
the world, he took an interest in politics, a
wanted to know what we were doing about Egy
However, he made up for that by selling us m
butter and potatoes, and he also gave me so
tobacco of his own growing, raw leaves not
dry, which I hung over the cabin lamp till th
crackled, and then broke them up and smol
them, and found them a very great deal bet
than no tobacco at all.

Our most interesting visitors, however, w
two seal-hunters from Runö. I saw them buffet
their way along the quay afar off, and knew
once what they must be. No other men wear p
homespuns bound with black and hairy seals
shoes. No other men go abroad with long telesco
and crooked sticks. No other men on reach
our woodpile would climb upon the top of
crouching low against the wind, and, steady
the end of the telescope by using the stick as
support, would search so patiently the dist
rocks. Presently they were close to us, and ste

by a thought.   The Ancient talked wi
and told me that they begged . . . fo
For glass bottles, the one thing they do 1
upon their island.   They needed bottles
for carrying water, for what not ?   We g&
a lot of empty beer-bottles.   They took
caps and shook our hands.   Then the
if they might come on board.   They c&
went down into the cabin, fingering ev
enormously, inarticulately interested.

"A strong ship," said the younger,
" We too have a strong ship, with five li
which she carries inside her."

" And where is your ship ? "

" Over there, a half-hour's walk, in
harbour than this."

" And are there five of you ? "

" Yes, five.   Three we left on an island
coast of Oesel, with their three boats.   We
two.   In four weeks we shall sail back a
Oesel coast and find our men, and then 1
Runö again."

" Have you got many seals ? "

" Only one.   The weather is too bad f(
but later we shall have more."

There was a little more simple quest
answer of this kind.   Then they saw my
and asked what it was.   I told them,
younger one understood at once, and s&
they had seen photographs that had bee

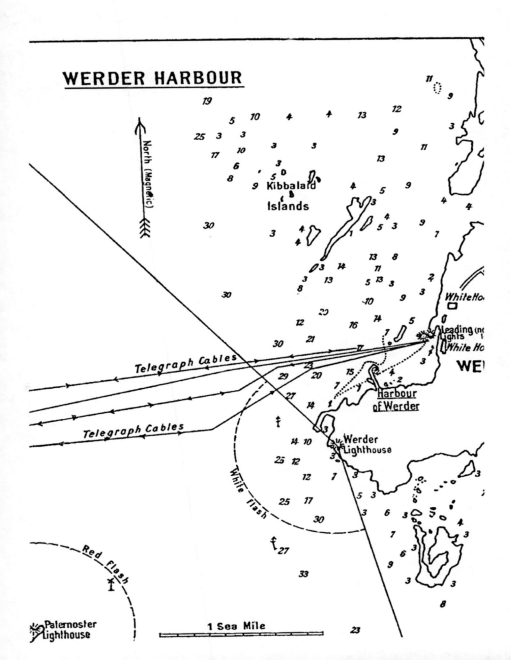

WERDER HARBOUR

but I told them that for picture-making I neec
a good light, and not a raging storm with wi
and hail. If it should clear later I would cor
With that we all gravely shook hands and th
went off.

SEAL-HUNTERS FROM RUN

SEPTEMBER 24TH. Last night we had a
taste of the Equinox in a northerly g
heavy rain. This morning, however, the
wind continued, the sky cleared, the su:
and I made up my mind to sail this ev
the weather held and the barometer, no
rising, did not take another dive. In tl
time I determined to use Sunday mor
repaying the visit of the men of Runö.
promised to photograph their ship.

I saw the men of Runö about a mile
shore, conspicuous in their pale homespu
slinging my camera on my back, was blo
the pier and almost off it as I hurried ir
of them. "These men live on a little
said I to myself, "therefore they cannot
walkers. At any rate I, who have spent
life afoot on the fells of England, ough
able to catch up with them." Catch the
but after a long struggle, though they did
to be hurrying. The older, shorter man w
his carved stick as a staff, the younger was
in his toes as he walked, and yet they ke

to see what they could gather from the pec
of the continent. When at last I caught th
they had stopped at one of the few inhabi
cottages, and the young one, after greeting
with joy and agreeing at once to take me to tl
ship, bitterly complained that the house was s
up and no one was at home. He pointed to
sun and to my camera case, remembering tha
had told him yesterday that I could photogrɛ
his ship only if there was a good sun.

We set off across country, the men of R
swearing that it was not far to the ship. We pas
through the grounds of a ruined country ho
a fine place before the war, but now a deso
shell; then out over wide marshland, and, a
half an hour's walking, they pointed to a w
mast against the shadow of a distant wood.
men of Runö and I walked our natural p
and the Esthonian boy trotted at our heels.
we walked we talked, a sort of Volapuk or Es
anto, composed of German, Swedish and Rus
words stirred well together with a lot of good
We understood one another excellently. T
explained that the rig of their boat was not
that of the Esthonians, but was a traditional
from older times than man can remember,
peculiar to Runö. They told me that they ha
fine gun, that there were pike in some water
the left of us, that they had shot some good d
in a bight on the other side, and so on. I

wind for Riga." I pointed to the clear b
overhead, but they would have none of it.
fran Runö kens wetter. Bettra i morgen.
fem segel. En gud wind till Riga," and
with such insistence that I made up my i
wait till morning and see if the men of Rur
the weather as well as they thought they c

Talking so, we came through a little v
a tiny natural harbour, where their ship
anchor, a strange ship indeed, bigger than *Rc*
but not much, with a long bowsprit, a fe
with a high spritsail, and a mainmast c
length, exactly in the middle of the ship,
marked rake towards the stern, a short g
a very long boom projecting far over the e
Drawn up on the grassy shore were tw
boats shaped like narrow spoons, that c
should think, be used either with oars or
single paddle like a canoe. I took a pho
of the ship as she lay there, with the littl
on the shore, and each man ran of his own
to be photographed each by his own littl
which, as they explained, each had ma
himself. The Esthonian boy wanted to be
graphed also, but they would have none
and drove him away, saying that he was n
Runö and therefore should not be in the
He ran off angrily into the woods, and we s
no more. Then we all three got into one
little boats, and the younger man ferried

SEAL HUNTERS, THEIR BOAT AND SHIP.

counter: "JUBA: RUNÖ." They brought
boat stern foremost under the counter and
scrambled up and in.

Whatever the *Juba* might want in cleanlin
and she wanted a good deal, she made up in streng
She was built in 1911 on Runö. The elder n
had taken part in the building. Her planking v
of oak, two inches thick, I judged, and her r
—square-sided ribs of ash or elm, I could not
certain from their description which they mean
were enormously heavy. The counter was partia
decked, the whole of the midships portion v
open, while the forepart of the ship was decl
over with a high curved roof, making a very roo
forecastle. In front of the mainmast were two
barrels, one full of seal-fat, the other of seal-fle
A skin was drying in the sun. In the covered fo
castle, a great space, bigger even than *Racundi*
prided cabin, were stowed a great mass of s
and all kinds of gear. They burrow under the s
to sleep. There were shelves along the sides w
rough wooden spoons and boxes which tl
decorate with fire, scraps of leather, partly m
shoes, hanks of yarn and fishing-tackle. Tl
brought out their seal-gun, a muzzle-loading fli
lock that might have been used by the Jacobi
They had made a case for it of sealskin with
hair outside. The elder man had also a Japan
rifle, but they both agreed that the ancient fl
was "bettra." I asked them if they were go

worked leather borders, very fine shoes
for this was Sunday, and just as to-d
were wearing the newest of pale homespun
with trousers like straight tubes to match,
were wearing new shoes, both shoes and
being identical with those they had worn y
except for their newness. Everything th
they had made themselves on the island or
ship, with the exception of their caps.   T.
had a cap of plain blue, the younger a Nev
check cloth cap, faded almost white, wi!
through which shreds of pink-silk lining
but still a fine thing from foreign parts a
with Sunday clothes in simple pride.

They told me they came every year
particular little inlet.   I asked how many
twenty ?   Far more.   The older man s¿
his father had brought him there the fi
he came.   I have no doubt that for not
twenty but for several hundred years
ship of strange rig has anchored there and
out of its hold the little spoon-shaped
boats, and simple men in pale clothes bou
black, with ornamental shoes of sealskin.
men, perhaps better than any other Eu
except the Laplanders, continue into ou
the life their forbears lived in the Midd
and earlier.   Steam has meant nothing t
except a visit from a steamboat once

heads without these things. One thing of r(
value to them dropped from civilisation th
had indeed upon the *Juba*, and they brought
to me in its box and opened its dark magic w:
proper reverence. It was an old dry compass fr(
a maker in Wapping, taken, no doubt, from so1
ship wrecked fifty years ago on the rocky weste
shores of their island.

We parted with high mutual esteem, express
by an exchange. I gave them the old pipe I w
smoking. The elder man gave me a worn tobac(
pouch. " Fran England till Runö. Fran Runö 1
England," he said, carefully stowing my pi
upon his crowded shelf. Then there was a trem(
dous handshaking and bowing and taking off
caps. After which the younger man took 1
ashore. I had got his name, and he begged 1
to send him the pictures, addressed simply " Are1
burg for Runö." " We shall get them next sumn
when the steamer comes."

WERDER TO RIGA

THE men of Runö were so far right that
hard during the night, though the storm t
expected was reserved for us on the nigh
In the morning of September 25th, at eight
the barometer was at 29.4, and at ten v
a point higher. For the first time for a f
it had been for forty-eight hours compa
steady, and not on the upward or downwai
of a steep switchback. The wind was N.V
little Russian steamer which, going sou
ourselves, had waited by Kuivast all the
day was getting her anchor. I had a feel
now was our chance, and that we had
take it before, as it were, the Equinox
second wind.

"What about sailing?" said I to the
who was on the pier sheltering behind th
pile and looking through the glasses at t
steamer.

"We can but try," said he.

And with that we began casting off the
web of stout warps with which we had been

snug below, and at 10.45 we had got our anc.
and were beating out into the Sound under bri
sunshine and a blue sky with racing clouds,
outlines of which encouraged us by being v
much softer than the oily, knife-edged affairs
the last few days. At a quarter past eleven
were close to the mouth of the Sound. Paternos
Lighthouse on Virelaid island, a compact li
hummock with rocks all round it and rock-l
haystacks on the low land behind it, bore W. by
We were level with the second Werder buoy,
open sea was before us, and I set our course due
which should give us a sight of Runö Lightho
to help us in the night. *Racundra* was going
grand pace, and our faith in the men of Ru
grew stronger every minute.

At one o'clock we sighted a steamer aste
coming out of the Sound and going S. She pas:
us several miles to eastward, very much disqui
ing the Ancient, who had never really trus
our compass after we had had its natural err
adjusted at Helsingfors.

"She'll be setting her course straight, and w
her leaving us to west like that, we shall be pass:
Runö on the wrong side and getting among th
shoals."

I had a hard job to persuade him that t
steamer might have her course and we might ha
ours and both of us be right. I showed him t
English mine-chart, with its swept channel for l

should shift again.   Also, the steamer':
would actually be longer than our own.
fessed himself satisfied, but was not, unti
the afternoon, when, while he and the Co
below and I was at the tiller, I saw sc
on the starboard bow that could not be
that was . . . no . . . yes, actually wa
Lighthouse. The lighthouse bore S.W. b
could not keep the triumph out of my
I shouted down the companion way, "
sight "; but that unbelieving Ancient,
came hurriedly up, stared over the port
moment his head was above the level of t
showing clearly what he had expected.

"Starboard bow," said I, " and pretty

" By gum, you were right !" said the
and the quarrel ended. More serious matt
on hand. *Racundra* was moving much
The men of Runö had been right about the
gale, but had expected it a day too so
even if we continued at the pace we were no
racing in a bath of foam, we should, I ca
be on the bar of Dvina about one in the r
Now, leading lights are delightful things
by, and in most circumstances a well-lit
is easier for a stranger by night than
But the entrance to the Dvina, child's
ordinary weather, is a most tricky busin
northerly winds. I quote from the *Balt*
" On the shoals which are steep to, there is

being a thoroughly unpleasant bit of work i
a little ship. On going out we had noticed
unlucky schooner which had failed to clear the
shoals and had been flung ashore on the weste
side of the river mouth. To-day, I knew that t
current would be setting the other way, but
had no sort of wish to see *Racundra* swept
either side of the entrance to her home port
the end of her first cruise, and preferred to ha
daylight so as to be better able to judge the s
and the current and to decide in time whether
keep the sea or run in.

Accordingly, we brought *Racundra* to the wi
and reefed her—reefed her relentlessly. It is
well-known fact that, while running before
you do not feel the wind. It was not until
stopped there, a dozen miles off Runö, and broug
Racundra up to face it, that we knew how stro
the wind had grown. We took in both the de
reefs in the mainsail, turning it into a thi
scarcely bigger than an afternoon tea cloth, a
then stripped her of her mizen. We left the stays
standing, arguing that it would not do mu
pulling with the wind aft, and yet would perha
hold a little wind in the troughs of the wav
even if the shortened mainsail should be who
becalmed. Further, it would be of extreme usef
ness if from some unpleasing accident we shou
happen to broach to. When all was done, I set
new course, S. by E., to bring us to the head

out admirably in practice. We then settl
for the night.

" Settled down " is perhaps not quite tl
to use, for nothing could be very settled i
sea as had got up. The Cook, for the first
the whole voyage, was in a state of colla
partly to the fumes of the raw tobacco dr}
the cabin lamp. The waves were so steep
actual pitching of the ship, the lift and
the rolling, was too much for the Primus
Nothing would stay on them. And .
seemed to be moving almost as fast a
we reefed her. The Ancient munched
swallowed raw eggs, and *Racundra* rush
over a dark sea with breaking waves, th
a stormy sunset in the west, on a green
patch of which we could just see the Ru:
house and the topmost trees of the island
us in the north were patches of starligh
as we watched them, were swept into l
and then everything went dark in a sudde
of rain. Then again were patches of
with huge clouds chasing small ones, ;
a great mass that seemed suddenly to
till the whole sky was gone and the l
rattled on the decks.

It was a weird, exciting night, but not
one, for we knew that the worst was l
that we were running for a lee-shore,
mistakes would be disastrous and that i

the autumn. "Especially during the autumn
the words of that pessimist *Baltic Pilot* glowe
dully before me, and I asked myself, half angril
why on earth I had not been content to fish f(
pike in England and to leave the Baltic to bett
men. And then, as always, *Racundra* comforte
me. She ran so steadily, steered so easily, w:
so much less flustered than her "master ar
owner" when, glancing back, he saw the horizo
apparently only a few yards off, rise astern lil
a white-topped mountain, up and up and u
and nearer and nearer, till it seemed that it mu
overwhelm her in its majestic rush. But *Racund*
kept quietly on her path, rose as the huge wa`
reached her, dropped down its mighty back, ar
was running still while the horizon heaved its(
again behind her for another effort.

Racundra, I say, comforted me. She seemed
have no doubts at all about what she could (
or couldn't. And I found myself slowly comin
to share her confidence. I sat with the tiller wedg(
between my left arm and my body, the han'
thrust each into the opposite sleeve of my oilskir
on account of the exceeding cold. The Ancie
crouched half-way down the companion way ar
disliked talking. At regular intervals we chang(
places, and he who was off duty sheltered in tl
companion way and tried to smoke the raw tobac(
of the Werder lighthouse-keeper, a kindly gi:
but a poor substitute for cut plug.

and more frequent glances over the side
electric torch on the foaming water, to
fast *Racundra* was going.   She was goi
too fast. We began to feel a special hati
dark.   It was as if someone had malici
the light out, and, with finger ready, wa
it out for our annoyance.   The nigh
unending.   And then, at three o'clock
unmistakably, the glow of Riga lights
port bow.   That, of course, was just w
should have been, but we should have
to see them an hour or two later.   Then
appeared, leaving us to suppose that we wei
into thick weather, when they would nc
at all and we should be in worse case.
hour later we saw them again, and after 1
wholly lost them.   They are supposed to
twenty-five miles.

We held on, with redoubled impatience
the eastern sky for the faintest promise
Imperceptibly, even to us watchers, the
difference in the darkness.   The horizon o
side was farther away.   On that side
actually see the waves, and the water,
been black as the night except for its whit
was now the colour of a pewter mug.

Some time before that we had sighted
buoy ten miles out from Riga, and h
pretty sharp demonstration of the stren

it, keeping the boat's nose on it whenever the wav
let us see it. Before we reached it, I asked h
again how it was bearing. He replied, " Sout
west by west." It is what is known in the
parts as a howling-buoy, and announces its opini
of its uncomfortable position by a long-drawn cr
between a groan and a whistle, as it lifts and fa
in the waves. As we passed it after thus learni
what sort of a current we had to contend wit
this melancholy noise expressed our own feelin
so perfectly that we had no need for words.

I decided to keep *Racundra* heading in such
way that a line between the howling-buoy's flas
light and the light from Riga should be to ea
of us, and to abandon the idea of getting in t
moment we should find ourselves unable to ke
on the right side of this imaginary line. After ha
an hour's rather anxious watching we were pret
well assured that we could do it, and when at la
it grew light, just before we reached the secor
buoy, which is two miles out from the mouth
the river, we were confident of being able to ste
the current and get in if it should not be reinforce
by some particular malice of the waves. Thes
of course, were much steeper as we approach
the bar, and we saw with some trepidation th
three steamships were waiting outside, the pil
having evidently refused to come out during tl
night. Land was, of course, visible now alike
east and west. We could see Riga town and tl

that we had noticed on our way out and t
white breakers storming the moles and
angrily up the shores on either side of the
Still, just as we passed the second buo:
green light already blinking palely in
daylight, we saw smoke in the mouth ol
and then the pilot tug coming out.   W
and lost her, saw her and lost her in
as we approached.   We passed her cle
she went to meet the steamers.   She was
literally half out of the water, and then,
down into a meeting wave, ceased to k
tug, but became a single splash, higher
own funnel top, like the splash of a]
hitting the water horizontally.   From I
some sort of idea of what *Racundra* must
like, though that stout little ship, run
the wind, was making much better wea
than the tug.   *Racundra* was steering e
took only a few slight splashes of watei
stern (I do verily believe that there is 1
beat the sharp-ended Scandinavian steri
ning in a seaway) as she raced one h
after another towards the river mou
mountain after another came up be
seemed for a moment to carry her upon it:
foaming crest, and left her to be carrie
by the next, while she, good little thing,
her best herself.
And now we were already in the narr

from her course. But *Racundra*, demure, det
mined, shouldered them good-temperedly aside a
held on. Almost before we knew it we were acr
the bar and in the entrance, watching with of
mouths the tiny boats of the fishermen, labour
with their nets in the huge swell that came
from the sea. A northerly storm brings the f
to the Dvina, and next day the market was full
big salmon, so that the fishermen were well rewarc
for their work. But *Racundra* is a lucky little sh
The night before, another boat, bigger than s
had tried to make the entrance, had failed, a
been smashed to pieces in a few minutes on t
eastern side of the river mouth. This we lea:
from the Customs officials who, while congra
lating us on getting in, now set about making
home-coming unpleasant.

Perhaps if we had been less tired and hung
their red-tape cobwebs, from which on going
we had been so happily excused, would not ha
annoyed us so much. And afterwards I felt inclir
to forgive them, when I learnt that they h
reason to believe that during the summer peo
had made use for smuggling of the privileges giv
by a yacht flag. Still, we were not smuggle
and, at the time, were very angry indeed.
had intended to sail straight up the river to
cleared in the Mühlgraben at the same Custo
station where we had been cleared when outw:
bound. This, however, did not suit the offic

sides with a big Customs House tug. Th
made me row back to their office, and I v
being swamped in *Racundra's* cockleshell
after *Racundra* herself had carried me :
Then they said that, after all, we might
directly to the Yacht Club with an excise
charge on board, and wait there until th
sent an official from Riga. I rowed ba
sulkily to the Winter Harbour, where
breakfast, serving out a tot of rum to the
man who was now our gaoler.

Then, under the mainsail, we tacked out
harbour and had a glorious run up the river
were many sailing vessels, schooners, ketch
a fine barquentine, waiting for better weatl
a favourable wind. We reached throu
Mühlgraben past the little yellow Customs
past the now vacant berth where the *l*
had been when we borrowed the lead, an
fully through the narrow channel into the St
In smooth water and with the wind aft, *R*
slid easily homewards past the well-known
marks, the old white boat high up on the
shore, the promontory of dark pine-trees
western; and, at half-past twelve on Sep
26th, rounded into the little sheltered l
where, five weeks earlier, the dallying car
had been expelled from her and she had ta
stores before starting on her cruise.

Three hours later a Customs officer and a

at their door and be cleared on the spot. They v
no less full of wrath than I, and, as our pa
were in order and we had drunk and eaten
smoked everything on board and so had notl
to declare, formalities were quickly over,
ensign hauled down, and *Racundra* was offici
at home to lay up for the winter.

APPENDIX

A DESCRIPTION OF "RACUNDRA

"RACUNDRA" is nine metres over all—something u
thirty feet long. She is three and a half metres in bea
about twelve feet. She draws three feet six inches wit
her centreboard, and seven feet six inches when the ce
board is lowered. Her enormous beam is balanced by
shallowness, and though for a yacht it seems exces
thoroughly justified itself in her comfort and stiffness.
has a staysail, mainsail and mizen, and for special occa
a storm staysail, a balloon staysail, a small squaresail (1
too small), a trysail and a mizen staysail. She could (
carry a very much greater area of canvas, but, for
venience in single-handed sailing, she has no bowsprit,
the end of the mizen boom can be reached from the
  She is very heavily built and carries no inside ba
Her centreboard is of oak. She has a three-and-a-ha
iron keel, so broad that she will rest comfortably up
when taking the mud, and deep enough to enable 1
do without the centreboard altogether except when sque
her up against the wind. Give her a point or two free
a good wind and her drift, though more than that
deep-keel yacht, is much less than that of the coa
schooners common in the Baltic. With the centre

But the chief glory of *Racundra* is her cabin. T
yachtsmen, accustomed to the slim figures of racin
jeered at *Racundra's* beam and weight, but one
when they came aboard her, ducked through the co
way and stood up again inside that spacious cabin
that there was something to be said for such a boa
as for their wives, they said frankly that such a cab
a boat worth having, and their own boats, wh
seemed comfortable enough hitherto, turned into n
comfortable rabbit-hutches. *Racundra's* cabin is
where a man can live and work as comfortably ar
as pleasantly as in any room ashore. I lived in it
months on end, and, if this were a temperate clim:
the harbour were not a solid block of ice in winter,
all yachts are hauled out and kept in a shed for
year, I should be living in it still. Not only can or
up in *Racundra's* cabin, but one can walk about th
that without interfering with anyone who may be
at the writing-table, which is a yard square. In the
of the cabin is a folding table, four feet by three, su
by the centre-board case; and so broad is the flc
you can sit at that table and never find the case in
of your toes. The bunks are wider than is usual,
hind and above each bunk are two deep cupboar(
between them a deep open space divided by a she
on the port side for books and on the starboard
crockery. Under the bunks is storage for bottles.
the flooring on the wide flat keel is storage for co
milk and tinned food. Behind the bunks, betwee
and the planking, below the cupboards and book
is further storage room.

APPENDIX

made me an admirable little three-legged stool, which,
the ship is under way, stows under the table. Above
behind the ample field of the table is a deep cupboard
a bookcase, of a height to take the *Nautical Almanack*
Admiralty Pilots, Dixon Kemp and Norie's inevitable *Ep*
and *Tables*. Another long shelf is to be put up along
bulkhead that divides the cabin from the forecastle. U
the shelf for nautical books is a shallow drawer whe
keep a set of pocket tools, nails, screws and such th
Under the writing-table is a big chart drawer, where I
the charts immediately in use, writing and drawing mate
parallel rulers, protractors, surveying compass, stopv
and other small gear. By the side of this is a long na
drawer, used for odds and ends, and underneath that
special cupboard made to take my portable typewriter.

On the starboard side, opposite the table is space
stove, which, however, on this cruise we used for sto
spare mattresses. Behind it are deep cupboards with
coamings to prevent things slipping. Here were e
portmanteaux, seaboots, and a watertight box for p
graphic material. The door into the forecastle is on
side, so that it is possible to go through even when son
is sitting at the writing-table. In the forecastle is
full-length comfortable bunk on the port side. On
starboard side there are big cupboards instead of a se
bunk. These were used for ship's stores, such as b
and carpenter's tools, shackles and the rest. A seat is
close by the mainmast, to a big central cupboard whi
the full height of the forecastle from deck to floor, and
used for oilskins and clothes. In the forecastle we st
warps, spare anchor, tins of kerosine, one of the water-b

As you come out of the cabin into the compar
you find on either hand a cupboard from deck to
the starboard side is a simple and efficient closet,
of that, under the deck, a big space used for all the er
tools, lubricating oils and greases. On the port si
galley, with room for three Primus stoves (I am
Clyde cooker). One of the stoves is in heavy iron
for use when under way. Behind this is a shelf
for cooking things, and aft, under the deck, a secor
barrel. The engine, a heavy oil, hot-bulb Swedis'
burning kerosine (we have no benzine on the ship),
the self-draining steering-well. It is completely
when not in use by a wooden case, contrived to pro\
up to the deck. The case takes to pieces, but can
with absolute rigidity, so that people who hav
Racundra have asked, on going away, what was the
of the reversing lever (at the side of the compar
within reach of the steering-well), never having
that we had an engine on board. For all the goo
of it during this first cruise we might just as well
no engine, but next year I hope to take the engine
and learn the Open Sesame that will set it miracu
work. The oil reservoir is in the extreme stern, and
from the deck. The companion way can be completel\
in by a folding and sliding lid, over which we sha
canvas cover. The raised wall of the cabin is car
pletely round companion, mizen mast and steerin\
that there is plenty of room inside this coaming fc
to lie full length. In summer this would be a most
place to sleep, and even on this autumn cruise, du
days of fine weather we put one of the spare m

APPENDIX

of the mizen mast, is the binnacle, and under the d
between companion way and steering-well, is a cupb
for riding light, binoculars, fog-horn, etc. The main sl
mizen sheet, backstays and staysail sheets are all cle
within easy reach of the steersman, who can do everyt
but reef without leaving his place. Owing to the he
of the narrow mainsail, inevitable in a ketch, the gaff t
to swing too far forward, so I have a vang, which also se
as a downhaul, fastened to the peak, and cleated, whe
use, close by the mizen mast.

British Sports Library

EDITED BY CAPTAIN F. A. M. WEBSTER, F.R.G.S.

Cr. 8vo.   *With Illustrations and Diagrams*   *6s. eac*

Vol. I. Rugby Football   By D. R. GENT

"A little square book packed tight as any Rugby scrummage itself coul
be packed with all the best wisdom and spirit of Rugby football. Th
invaluable little book—invaluable for anyone who would learn simply an
directly from a master of the craft the obvious yet subtle secrets of Rugb
football. What is so good about this book is that there is no ' flummery
. . . it goes straight for the goal, always trying to gain ground. H
gives hints that . . . even the cleverest Rugbeian hardly can afford t
miss."—*Westminster Gazette.*

Vol. II. Hockey   By S. H. SHOVELLER

"For the modest sum of 6s. can be purchased all the skill, experienc
and the ripe wisdom of the greatest Centre Forward and player the gam
has ever produced. The player who could read this book and no
immensely benefit thereby would need to be extraordinarily lacking i
perception and receptiveness. Every school and training college in th
land should place a copy of S. H. Shoveller's masterpiece in its library."-
Hockey Field.

Matahari : Impressions of the Siamese-Malayan Jungle

By H. O. MORGENTHALER

La. Cr. 8vo.   *Illustrated*   *7s. 6*

This Jungle Book of a Swiss mountaineer and geologist is not a
ordinary book of travels through wild and unknown countries, but i
interesting in the first place because its author is a man of humour fo
whom the lust of wandering and the joy in the beauty of the world ar
the foundation of all philosophy.

The personal note of the book, the way in which Morgenthaler looks a
Eastern things, the manner in which he makes the reader acquainte
with the strange features of Further India, all these give charm t
the book. The author's work brought him, as he himself says, " righ
into the heart of things," so that he is able to give the reader pictures c
Siamese and Malay life such as few white men can give.

Wanderings in the Queensland Bush

By W. LAVALLIN PUXLEY

Some Impressions of
Elders

By St. JOHN ERVINE

Cr. 8vo.

In this informal book of essays, Mr. Ervine mingles cri
appreciation. His " Elders " are " A.E." (the Irish po
William Russell), Arnold Bennett, G. K. Chesterton, John
George Moore, Bernard Shaw, H. G. Wells and W. B. Yea
Ervine writes of them and of their work in terms of int
asserts that they were, in varying degrees, among th
influences on "the young men of my generation "—the
who went to the war. The dominant of these influencing
Bernard Shaw and H. G. Wells, whose social and religio
are here expounded, not only as they agree, but as they
book is discursive, but never irrelevant, and Mr. Ervine ha
aspects of his " Elders " which have, perhaps, not previously b
The book abounds with incidental references to other writ
John Millington Synge, some of whom are described in
sentence such as that in which Mr. James Joyce is described a
after a nervous breakdown." The book will be found unusua
ing to all those who are attracted by the intellectual activ
present time and the past twenty years.

The Nineteen Hundr
By REGINALD AUBERON

Demy 8vo.

" It gives us a living, breathing picture of the way
(not necessarily nonentities) lived in a spacious and comfortal
that vanished in 1914. It is a picture of London life as it was
is why when much more pretentious autobiographies hav
into the waste-paper basket of oblivion it will be read with
Morning Post.

Oxford Oddities
By V. J. SELIGMAN
Author of " The Salonica Sideshow," etc.

Forty Years of Diplomacy

By BARON ROSEN

Demy 8vo. 2 VOLS. 25s. the s[...]

"To the student of the affairs of the last forty years the book will invaluable, for in it European politics are regarded by a trained observ from an angle that has all the charm of unfamiliarity."—*Daily Telegraf*

The Memoirs of an Ambassador

By FREIHERR VON SCHOEN

Demy 8vo. TRANSLATED BY CONSTANCE VESEY 10s. 6

"Freiherr von Schoen has written a dignified and candid account his experiences. . . . His sober and obviously honest description of t' chief events in which he played an important part is a valuable additi to the sources from which the future historian will compile his narrative —*Saturday Review.*

Sir William Wedderburn and the Indian Reform Movemen

By S. K. RATCLIFFE

Cr. 8vo.

Sir William Wedderburn was for over thirty years the most disti guished representative in England of the Indian Reform Party. I was for twenty-seven years a member of the Indian Civil Service, risi to high office in Bombay. He was a friend and devoted adherent Lord Ripon and laboured as a pioneer in vital measures of self-gover ment and rural reconstruction that have in later years been carried in effect. In the 'nineties he was "Member for India" at Westminste This memoir gives the history of the movement with which he was iden fied, and traces Wedderburn's work for the cause of India from the four ation of the Indian National Congress, through the stage of the Morl reforms, to the war and the shaping of the Montagu Act.

The Story of a Varied Life

An Autobiography

By W. S. RAINSFORD

Royal 8vo. 1[...]

Dr. Rainsford is best known in America as the great preacher, reform hunter, traveller, and friend of humanity who built up, as Rector of [...]

An Indiscreet Chronicle the Pacific By PUTNAM WEALE

Author of "The Truth About China and Japan," etc.,

Demy 8vo. *With Maps*

The author has lived in China since childhood, and for more years has held official positions of high importance in Government. In 1921 he undertook a confidential mission visiting Canada, the United States and then Europe, return Washington as one of the advisers of the Chinese Delegatio armament Conference. It is no exaggeration to state that Pu knows more of the confidential secrets of Far Eastern polit other Westerner, and in the present book he discloses man have until this time been kept *sub rosa.*

China in The Family Nations By DR. HENRY T. HOL

Author of "The Christian Revolution," "Lay:

Cr. 8vo.

After reviewing the history of China in her internatio ships, the author (who has had some twenty years' i varied experience of the country) attempts to show wha means for China herself and for the rest of mankind. He international situation, the industrial development of China a Thought Movement, and seeks throughout to present the ca in a sympathetic way.

The Problem of Chi By BERTRAND RUSSELL, F.R

La. Cr. 8vo.

" Few have brought to their task a more exquisite sensit swifter, stronger understanding."—*Daily Herald.*

"A stimulating contribution to our understanding of these O of civilization."—*Times.*

The Far Eastern Rep of Siberia By HENRY KITTRE NORTON

Demy 8vo.

This is the first unbiassed and authoritative account of wh happening during the last four years in the Far Eastern po

The League of Nations To-day

Its Growth, Record and Relation to Briti[sh] Foreign Policy

Cr. 8vo.   By ROTH WILLIAMS

This book aims to give an authoritative presentment of the existi[ng] League as an instrument issued from the play of certain kinds of pub[lic] opinion and foreign policy during the last few years, and makes concr[ete] suggestions for the perfection and use of this instrument in readj[ust]ing the relations between Great Britain and the Dominions and Gr[eat] Britain, India and Egypt; for inducing America to co-operate w[ith] Europe; for achieving full political and financial settlement between [the] Allies and Germany and Russia; and for the civilization of patriotism.

War : Its Nature, Cause an[d] Cure

By G. LOWES DICKINSON
Author of "The Choice before Us," etc.

Cr. 8vo.   4s. 6[d.]

This is a book of propaganda addressed to the plain man. It sho[ws] that war with modern weapons cannot be waged on a great scale with[out] destroying civilization and mankind. It shows also that the real cau[ses] of war are always the desires of some states, or of all states, to steal ter[ri]tory, markets and concessions. It analyses, in this sense, the causes of t[he] late war. And it appeals to the ordinary citizen to come out on the s[ide] of ending war if he wants to prevent the ending of mankind.

England Under Edward VI

Demy 8vo.   By J. A. FARRER   10s. 6[d.]

"The book is fresh and timely, and by dealing almost exclusively w[ith] the foreign situation Mr. Farrer adopts a method not usual w[ith] historians."—*Foreign Affairs.*

The Falsifications of the Russian Orange Book

With a Foreword by G. P. GOOCH

Demy 8vo.   2s. 6[d.]

Eight years after the publication of the Russian Orange Book we lea[rn] that the telegrams exchanged between Paris and Petrograd were

The Decay of Capit
Civilisation

By SIDNEY and BEATRICE WE

Cr. 8vo. *Cloth, 4s. 6d.;*

" Every Socialist will want to thank them for this book."-
" The case against Capitalist Civilisation is argued with
and wealth of illustrations."—*Observer.*

International Aspects
Unemployment

By Prof. WATSON KIRKCONNELL
University of Manitoba

Cr. 8vo.

No problem to-day has greater significance than unempl<
book by a Canadian publicist treats the phenomenon as a<
harmonies and hazards in our whole international civilizatio
premonitory plea for world co-operation.

The Economics of
Unemployment

J. A.

Cr. 8vo.

"Combines once more the rare virtues of conciseness,
authority. . . . The book demands, by the clearness of its
the persuasiveness of its argument, the careful attentio<
concerned over the serious problem with which it deals.
Guardian.

Stabilisation

An Economic Policy for Producers and C

By E. M. H. LLOYD

Cr. 8vo.

" A book that everyone concerned in finding the solution
chaos in trade and industry should study carefully."—*Outlc*

CPSIA information can be obtained at www.ICGtesting.com
Printed in the USA
LVOW100734211212

312526LV00004B/641/P